NOTABLE ACQUISITIONS

at the Art Institute of Chicago

Executive Director of Publications: Robert V. Sharp; Editors: Gregory Nosan and Amy R. Peltz; Designer: Jeffrey D. Wonderland; Production: Sarah E. Guernsey, Kate Kotan, and Carolyn Ziebarth; Photo Editor: Joseph Mohan; Subscription and Circulation: Bryan D. Miller and Molly Heyen.

This publication was typeset in Topaz and Stempel Garamond; color separations were made by Professional Graphics, Rockford, Illinois. Printed by Meridian Printing, East Greenwich, Rhode Island.

Distributed by Yale University Press, New Haven and London www.yalebooks.com

This publication is volume 35, number 2 of *Museum Studies*, which is published semiannually by the Art Institute of Chicago Publications Department, 111 South Michigan Avenue, Chicago, Illinois, 60603-6404.

For information on subscriptions and back issues, consult www.artic.edu/aic/books/msbooks or contact (312) 443-3786 or pubsmus@artic.edu.

Ongoing support for *Museum Studies* has been provided by a grant for editorial development and production, and from the Andrew W. Mellon Foundation.

This book was produced using paper certified by the Forest Stewardship Council.

ISSN 0069-3235
ISBN 978-0-86559-236-0

ART
INSTITVTE
CHICAGO

CONTENTS

FOREWORD AND ACKNOWLEDGMENTS

THE PERIOD FROM 2007 to 2009 has been a momentous one for the Art Institute of Chicago, marked by the completion and opening of the Modern Wing, the largest addition to the museum since the opening of our original Michigan Avenue structure in 1893. At 264,000 square feet, the new building has allowed us to add more classrooms for education and more galleries for modern and contemporary art, architecture, and design. But it has also permitted us to increase the gallery space devoted to the rest of the collection, much of which has been recently reinstalled. This issue of *Museum Studies* presents over forty of the most significant acquisitions made during the course of these past three years. We hope it will encourage readers to visit and see these changes for themselves, and while doing so to not only consider the holdings of each curatorial department separately, but also to take advantage of the encyclopedic nature of the museum and find unexpected connections and contrasts among diverse works, many of which attest to the varied forms of power that beautiful objects have held—and conferred—in different times and places.

Consider, for instance, a Maya blackware vessel from the Early Classic period (A.D. 250/450) that was produced by an artist who lived in what is today Guatemala. Its top is decorated with a large-beaked bird, while its body is supported by four legs that suggest wild pigs standing on their snouts. Compare this to a Chinese wine container made one thousand years earlier, during the Western Zhou dynasty (c. 1050–771 B.C.). Like the Maya vessel, it is adorned with bird motifs: in this case, heraldic, flamboyantly plumed creatures shown in profile. The precise functions of these objects and the purpose of their decorations differed. But both certainly enlivened the world of their makers, patrons, or recipients, conferring authority and dignity on the people and rituals they served.

Elsewhere in this volume appear three ceramic vases, all made in the early twentieth century by American potteries that were inspired by the artistic and social reforms of the Arts and Crafts movement, which embraced handcraftsmanship, the unity of design and material, and the rehabilitative effects of labor. Unlike the Maya and Zhou vessels, these derived their decorative motifs from plant forms—long-stemmed flowers and gracefully spiraling leaves. And we know their function: they were made to be sold commercially for domestic use. But even so, with their grace and delicate ornamentation, they added beauty to their surroundings, demonstrating their owners' refinement and membership in an aristocracy of taste—a different brand of prestige, but prestige nonetheless.

Consider, too, one final pair: the extraordinary Whitfield Cup and the bold and surprising *Object* by the French Surrealist Claude Cahun. Made in England in 1590, the Whitfield Cup consists of gilt silver and an ostrich egg. At the time, such eggs were thought to be laid by the griffin, a mythical beast. The magic of such a pedigree—and the fact that the cup may have been commissioned by Queen Elizabeth herself—surely conferred distinction on the person who possessed this object, and even today we wonder at the luxuriousness of its materials and manufacture. By contrast, Cahun's assemblage is made of ordinary found objects and constructed components, including a doll's hand and a tennis ball on which an eye has been painted. It suggests none of the delicate and rare craftsmanship of the cup, yet it too is mysterious. The artist herself called this piece and others like it "irrational" objects, works whose power resided in their capacity to create a rupture in the normal order of things.

While these pieces—and the many others published in this issue—each had a particular meaning and force in their original contexts, in their present surroundings they still exert a near-magical hold on our attention thanks to their beauty and history—a hold that is amplified by their new proximity to one another in the museum's galleries and within these pages. It is the purpose of encyclopedic museums such as the Art Institute to acquire, conserve, and present such works, making the power they possess available to all. This requires constant decisions as to which among the many pieces available to us at any given time should be brought into the museum's holdings. No other type of institution undertakes this task, and we assume it with enthusiasm and a grave sense of responsibility. Now, thanks to the opening of the Modern Wing—a magical work of art in its own right—visitors have the opportunity to enjoy a greater portion of these riches at any given time.

Like many projects at the Art Institute, this publication is the product of the combined efforts and expertise of staff throughout the museum. First and foremost, thanks go to the following scholars, who exercised their powers of discernment to research, acquire, and write about the works published here: Kathleen Bickford Berzock, Elizabeth Irene Pope, and Richard Townsend in the Department of African and Amerindian Art; Sarah E. Kelly, Ellen E. Roberts, and Brandon K. Ruud in the Department of American Art; Joseph Rosa and Zoë Ryan in the Department of Architecture and Design; Madhuvanti Ghose, Mary Greuel, Janice Katz, and Elinor Pearlstein in the Department of Asian and Ancient Art; Jenny Gheith and James Rondeau in the Department of Contemporary Art; Christopher Monkhouse in the Department of European Decorative Arts; Gloria Groom and Jill Shaw in the Department of Medieval through Modern European Painting and Sculpture; Katherine Bussard and Matthew S. Witkovsky in the Department of Photography; Jay A. Clarke, Suzanne Folds McCullagh, Mark Pascale, Martha Tedeschi, and Emily Vokt Ziemba in the Department of Prints and Drawings; and Odile V. Joassin in the Department of Textiles.

Books are magical objects in their own right, and producing them requires unique powers as well. For their patience and resourcefulness, we are grateful to longtime *Museum Studies* editor Greg Nosan, who expertly guided Amy R. Peltz through her first experience editing the journal, as well as to the talented production team of Sarah Guernsey, Kate Kotan, and Joseph Mohan, all of the Publications Department. We are also indebted to Christopher Gallagher, Robert Hashimoto, Robert Lifson, Loren McDonald, and Caroline Nutley in the Department of Imaging for their beautiful photographs of pieces in the Art Institute's collection; and, in the Graphics Department, to Jeffrey Wonderland, whose design of the volume shows each work of art to best effect. Once again, the staff of the museum has demonstrated that the institution's power lies not only in the strength of its collection, but also in that of its people.

JAMES CUNO
President and Eloise W. Martin Director

Vessel with Bird and Peccary Heads

A.D. 250/450

Early Classic Maya; Petén region, Guatemala

Ceramic and pigment; 24.8 x 25.4 cm (9 ¾ x 10 in.)

JOANNE M. AND CLARENCE E. SPANJER AND AFRICAN AND AMERINDIAN
CURATOR'S DISCRETIONARY FUNDS; O. RENARD GOLTRA AND NATIONAL
DOCENT SYMPOSIUM ENDOWMENTS; AFRICAN AND AMERINDIAN ART
PURCHASE FUND; DAVID SOLTKER AND IRVING DOBKIN ENDOWMENTS,
2008.206

THIS BEAUTIFULLY MODELED and incised blackware vessel was likely once the personal possession of a Maya king, who may have used it to serve food at royal feasts or who may have presented it as a gift to a visiting lord as a sign of alliance.[1] Its shape—a lidded dish supported by four legs—was a form frequently produced during the Early Classic period (A.D. 250/450).[2] These ceramics often display a consistent set of motifs, with birds on their domed lids and inverted peccary (wild pig) heads serving as supports. The artist who created this piece integrated the two-dimensional surface of the lid with its three-dimensional handle by connecting the bird's spread wings, incised into the surface, with its head, sculpted in the round. The vessel thus captures the essence of an aquatic bird floating on the surface of the water with its prey—a small fish—caught in its open beak.

Water birds and peccaries inhabited the natural landscape of the ancient Maya, who associated them with the structure of the universe and the time of creation. The crest of feathers atop the bird's head, its outstretched wings, and the bulge at the tip of its beak mark it as a cormorant.[3] The Maya regarded this bird as a liminal being, able to traverse three distinct environments: it flies in the sky, perches on land, and hunts fish by swimming deep under water. This was considered extraordinary, signifying the capacity to commune with supernatural beings that inhabit all three layers of the cosmos—a power that Maya kings also claimed to possess. The cormorant bore many additional meanings with which these rulers wished to link themselves—for example, its association with watery realms alludes to fertility and agricultural abundance, which kings needed to ensure so that their communities would survive. Water also evoked the distant mythological past, a time before the creation of the present universe when, according to Maya belief, everything was enveloped in a vast sea.[4] The peccaries furthered these cosmic associations as they are thought to have represented the four pillars that support the corners of the world.[5] In addition, some Maya identified clusters of stars in the constellation Gemini as peccaries.[6] This constellation is located in the region of the night sky where the seminal event of Maya creation—the resurrection of the maize god—was believed to have occurred.[7]

All of these formal and iconographic features demonstrate that, as a vessel made for a ruler and used in his court, this work was adorned with imagery designed to express the supernatural sources of his royal authority. In their art programs, Maya kings often associated themselves with the cosmos and the time of creation, thereby affirming that their right to rule was inherent in the world and was established at the beginning of time.

ELIZABETH IRENE POPE

Headdress for Gelede (Igi)

Early/mid-20th century

Attributed to Fagbite Asamu (active late 19th/mid-20th century) or Falola Edun (active early/mid-20th century)
Yoruba
Idahin, Ketu region, Republic of Benin

Wood and pigment; 40 x 36.8 x 48.9 cm (15 ¾ x 14 ½ x 19 ¼ in.)

GIFT OF NEAL BALL, 2008.176

AMONG THE YORUBA people of Republic of Benin and Nigeria, it is said that "the eyes that have seen Gelede have seen the ultimate spectacle."[1] Gelede is a dazzling series of events featuring daytime and nighttime masquerade performances by men wearing colorful costumes and elaborately sculpted wooden headdresses. This highly inventive example was likely made by Fagbite Asamu or his son Falola Edun, who were known for the vitality of their compositions. Gelede festivals are staged in towns and cities to honor the spiritual powers of female ancestors, deities, and elders—known collectively as "our mothers"—and to entertain them so that the community may benefit from their supernatural gifts. Oral history suggests that Gelede originated in the western Yoruba kingdom of Ketu during the eighteenth century, and today, it continues to be practiced primarily in the Ketu region, which straddles the Republic of Benin and Nigeria.

In its eye-pleasing masquerades, Gelede uses playacting and ribald humor to amuse and enlighten its audience. The men perform in pairs accompanied by a chorus of singing and drumming. Their costumes and dance steps often exaggerate the attributes and movements of womanly bodies. Accordingly, the base of each headdress depicts a female face with stylized features including almond-shaped eyes, a flared nose, shapely lips, and lines of scarification on the cheeks. Above this appears an endless array of imagery that encapsulates and interprets the Yoruba universe.

The figures that animate the superstructure of this headdress are depicted in a moment of tense uncertainty.[2] Will the precariously balanced pair of hunters, their legs entwined, capture the pangolin, a type of scaly anteater, or will the creature escape their grasp? The scene evokes a fundamental struggle between human intelligence and animal force, daring viewers to guess at the outcome of the battle. Frozen in time, the conflict recalls life's uncertainty and expresses a distinctly Yoruba worldview in which cosmic balance is maintained through the dynamic interplay of opposites.

An abbreviated Gelede festival can be held whenever needed, although many communities stage a large version at least once a year. Unlike Yoruba masquerades such as Egungun, which manifest powerful forces from the otherworld, Gelede is strongly tied to the earthly realm of human social interactions. Therefore, performers do not rigorously conceal their identities or wear potentially dangerous herbal medicines attached to their costumes, nor is proximity to them strictly controlled; rather, everybody in the community is welcome to enjoy the robust entertainment.

KATHLEEN BICKFORD BERZOCK

Snake Headdress (A-Mantsho-ña-Tshol *or* Inap)

Late 19th/early 20th century
Baga, Nalu, Landuma, Pukur, or Buluñits
Republic of Guinea
Wood and pigment; h. 205.7 cm (81 in.)

GIFT OF MURIEL KALLIS NEWMAN, 2007.572

INCREDIBLY, THIS TOWERING sculpture of a snake was made to be a headdress, lashed to a conical framework of palm branches and balanced atop a dancer's head. Below the snake, colorful cloths and palm fibers were hung in a dense fringe that completely concealed the dancer's body.[1] One elderly man described his experience of wearing such a headdress:

It was heavy and long. To put it up required four people, two on each side, in order to load it on. Once you could sense that it was in, and comfortable, you would signal to the four people to release it . . . In my quartier, I was the only one to carry it, because it was necessary to be physically strong, for it was heavy and extremely high . . . I bore it and I danced. It was not everyone who could bear it.[2]

As these recollections underscore, performing in the snake headdress required extraordinary strength and balance. The dancer's movements were sharp and quick; he dipped and rotated the headdress by bending at the knees and turning at the waist. It was a performance intended to inspire awe.

The snake masquerade was one of many traditions that migrated with the ancestors of the Baga and related peoples from the mountainous Fouta Djallon to the swampy Atlantic coast of what is now the Republic of Guinea beginning in the fifteenth century. Once established on the coast, the snake spirit became associated with the swamp-dwelling boa constrictor spirit, who blesses humankind with rain, fertility, and wealth.[3] The snake masquerade was often performed during initiation rites for young men, who then gained increased access to sacred knowledge. It could also form part of ritualized competitions between clans. Such performances were widespread in the region until the mid-1950s, when Islamic revolutionaries led a campaign to consolidate the religious and national identity of the nascent Republic of Guinea by suppressing diverse cultural practices.[4]

Longtime Art Institute of Chicago benefactor and trustee Muriel Kallis Newman gave this snake headdress to the museum shortly before her death in 2008.[5] She was perhaps most renowned for her collection of New York School paintings, many purchased directly from artists such as Jasper Johns and Mark Rothko in the 1950s and early 1960s. However, Newman also collected notable African works during these years, when Baga ritual sculpture first entered the art market due to the social upheaval that preceded Guinea's independence.[6] Newman's attraction to the snake headdress is unsurprising given her taste in modern art. The scale, simplicity of form, and bold patterning of Baga serpent headdresses resonated with the stripped-down minimalism then developing among New York artists.[7]

KATHLEEN BICKFORD BERZOCK

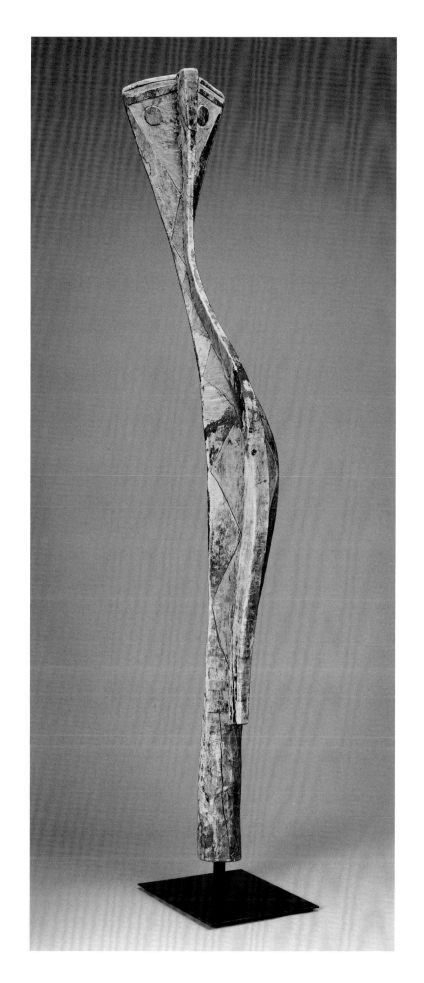

Polychrome Jar

C. 1954

Frog Woman (Joy Navasie) (Hopi-Tewa, born 1919)
Arizona, United States

Ceramic and pigment; 22.9 x 38.1 cm (9 x 15 in.)

GIFT OF DAVID AND CINDY VAN ZELST, 2008.178

THIS EARTHENWARE VESSEL has a flawless shape that gracefully curves from the upper rim to the swelling shoulder, with a long downward sweep to the foot; the smooth burnished surface displays a colorful pattern of symbolic motifs. Although made in the 1950s, the work belongs to a ceramic tradition that began in the greater Southwest almost two thousand years ago. In that remote archaeological past, pottery making spread throughout a region embracing southern Arizona and parts of Sonora and Chihuahua, Mexico, and northward along the rugged Mogollon Rim and across the Colorado Plateau to the Rio Grande Valley in New Mexico. Scores of individual and collective styles took form over the centuries, as potters from different communities created a diversity of revivals; mutations occurred; and old forms were displaced by new ones. Yet this ongoing process was always part and parcel of a widely shared artistic and cultural tradition.[1]

Around the turn of the twentieth century, a Hopi-Tewa lineage of artists began giving fresh impetus to this ancient legacy. The celebrated Nampeyo and her contemporaries were inspired by shapes and graphic forms on archaeological vessels and fragments being excavated from ruins near their desert mesa villages, or pueblos, of Hano, Sichomovi, and Walpi. This rediscovery sparked a revival, with the most imaginative artists using the ancient shapes and design motifs as points of departure for creating their own inventive forms.[2]

By the 1950s, Frog Woman (Joy Navasie), a member of this lineage, had become an outstanding potter. Her hallmark wares feature a background of white slip, or liquid clay, animated by asymmetrical patterns of winglike forms, stylized feathers, angular stepped motifs, and cosmological signs, all associated with rain, fertility, and seasonal regeneration. Such themes also appear in the artistic vocabularies of many other Southwestern Pueblo potters. Today, more than a century after the revival began, Frog Woman is a respected elder among the younger artists who continue producing wares that are highly prized by museums and collectors. Yet the making of ceramics, like many other aspects of Pueblo Indian culture, remains deeply connected to ancient beliefs in a supernatural order. Clay itself has life, and a sacred relationship begins for the potter when the clay is taken from the earth and thanks are offered to Earth Clay Old Lady. From this perspective, the potter's work is seen as a reflection of life forces, and the vessels are reminders that every aspect of our existence is part of an interpenetrating cosmic system.

RICHARD TOWNSEND

The Prairie on Fire

1827

Alvan Fisher (American, 1792–1863)

Oil on canvas; 61 x 83.8 cm (24 x 33 in.)

Signed, dated, and inscribed: *Painted by Alvan Fisher 1827* (on verso, underneath lining)

THROUGH PRIOR ACQUISITION OF THE GEORGE F. HARDING FUND; RESTRICTED GIFT OF JAMEE J. AND
MARSHALL FIELD; AMERICANA FUND, 2008.559

IN 1829, THE AMERICAN sculptor Horatio Greenough reported: "A little new year's
book has arrived here in which is an engraving from Mr F—'s prairie on fire. Mr Cooper
said twas the best—the only good illustration he had seen from his books."[1] The painting
James Fenimore Cooper admired was Alvan Fisher's *The Prairie on Fire*. Inspired by
Cooper's 1827 novel *The Prairie*—the third of his five *Leatherstocking Tales*—Fisher's
painting is the Art Institute's first depiction of a Cooper subject, as well as its first work
by this significant early American landscapist.

A native of the Boston area, Fisher made his living through portraiture but preferred
to paint landscapes.[2] When he traveled to Europe in 1825, he especially admired J. M. W.
Turner's work and collected prints after the English artist's paintings.[3] In *The Prairie on
Fire*, Fisher adopted Turner's loosely painted, atmospheric style as well as his Romantic-
era interest in dramatic scenes featuring striking contrasts between light and dark.

The painting corresponds to the following passage from Cooper's *The Prairie*: "'Now,'
said the old man, holding up a finger and laughing in his peculiarly silent manner, 'you
shall see fire fight fire!'"[4] At center, Natty Bumppo, the hero of all the *Leatherstocking
Tales*, has created a firebreak to save the story's protagonists. Inez Middleton and Ellen
Wade are draped in blankets to protect them from the fire, Duncan Middleton wears an
army officer's uniform, and Bumppo and Paul Hover are clad in frontier clothing, details
that mark the setting as American. By depicting Bumppo in mid-gesture with the other
characters looking on, Fisher identified him as the scene's pivotal character.

The painting differs from contemporaneous illustrations of this incident, which give
little sense of the setting.[5] Perhaps Cooper admired Fisher's work because it successfully
conveyed the prairie's importance in his text. Just as the author repeatedly described that
landscape's desolation, the artist portrayed the figures dwarfed by nature's expanse. He
also rendered the grasses with exquisite care, underscoring this environment's beauties as
well as its dangers.

One year after he painted it, Fisher sold this work to the writer and editor Samuel G.
Goodrich for one hundred dollars.[6] An important patron of the artist, Goodrich published
Elisha Gallaudet's engraving after the picture in his periodical *The Token*, where Cooper
saw it. Famed in its time, *The Prairie on Fire* is a significant early landscape by a pioneer
in the genre, a man whose work greatly influenced the next generation of American
landscapists, the Hudson River School.

ELLEN E. ROBERTS

Three Vases

1903/09

Design attributed to George Prentiss Kendrick (American, 1850–1919)
Decorated by Eva Russell (American, active c. 1905)
Grueby Faience Company (1894–1909), Boston, Massachusetts

Glazed earthenware; 37.5 x 20.3 x 20.3 cm (14 ³⁄₄ x 8 x 8 in.)

Marked: *GRUEBY•POTTERY BOSTON • U•S•A* (on bottom in circle with centered lotus blossom); *5/25; ER*

RESTRICTED GIFT OF THE ANTIQUARIAN SOCIETY; THROUGH PRIOR ACQUISITION OF THE B. F. FERGUSON FUND; ROGER AND J. PETER MCCORMICK, AND WESLEY M. DIXON, JR., ENDOWMENTS; THROUGH PRIOR ACQUISITION OF THE ANTIQUARIAN SOCIETY; GOODMAN, SIMEON B. WILLIAMS, HARRIET A. FOX, AND MRS. WENDELL FENTRESS OTT FUNDS; HIGHLAND PARK COMMUNITY ASSOCIATES; CHARLES R. AND JANICE FELDSTEIN ENDOWMENT FUND FOR DECORATIVE ARTS, 2008.558

C. 1909

Designed by Annie E. Aldrich (American, 1857–1937)
Made by John Swallow (born England, active c. 1910)
Decorated by Sarah Tutt (American, 1859–1947)
Marblehead Pottery (1904–36), Marblehead, Massachusetts

Glazed earthenware; 21.6 x 17.5 x 17.5 cm (8¹⁄₂ x 6 ⁷⁄₈ x 6 ⁷⁄₈ in.)

Marked: *M* and *P* flanking a sailboat at sea within a circle (on bottom); *A* and *T* (below this)

VANCE AMERICAN FUND; RESTRICTED GIFT OF THE ANTIQUARIAN SOCIETY, 2008.74

C. 1905

Designed by Fritz Albert (American, born Alsace-Lorraine, 1865–1940)
Gates Potteries, a division of the American Terra Cotta and Ceramic Company (1887–c. 1930), Terra Cotta, Illinois

Glazed earthenware; 45.7 x 15.9 x 15.9 cm (18 x 6 ¹⁄₄ x 6 ¹⁄₄ in.)

Marked: *TECO* (twice, on bottom); *310* (model number)

PROMISED GIFT OF CRAB TREE FARM FOUNDATION, 557.2005

DURING THE LATE nineteenth and early twentieth centuries, the United States witnessed the rise of several potteries that either embraced or reinterpreted the artistic and social reforms of the Arts and Crafts movement. Grueby Faience Company, Marblehead Pottery, and Gates Potteries—the firms responsible for the three extraordinary examples here—all looked to the natural world for aesthetic inspiration, and while both Grueby and Marblehead embraced the movement's plea for handcrafting as a solution to industrialization, Gates adopted machinery to reach a wide audience. William H. Grueby started his firm in Boston in 1894, and by 1897, draftsman and metalworker George Prentiss Kendrick had joined the company. Kendrick introduced sophisticated floral applications into the repertoire, adapting elegant foliage to Grueby's muscular vessels. On the Art Institute's piece (left), Japanesque design elements are evoked by the organization of the elongated daffodil stems into neat rows and by the vase's color and shape; the exquisitely curled petals, which intricately fold over and under one another, indicate a highly skilled decorator.[1] In its promotional literature, the firm emphasized the "touch of the artist's hand," and at Grueby, handcrafting reached near-cult status.[2] The company's devotion to time-consuming applied decoration, however, also spelled its demise.[3]

William Day Gates launched production of Teco, a contraction of the word *terra-cotta*, in 1899, in direct competition with firms such as Grueby. Gates marketed his wares as an alternative to more expensive handcrafted pottery, and the company embraced methods of mass-production, including casting.[4] The fame of Teco's products rested not on their surface decoration but on their innovative shapes and crystalline glazes. To create unique forms, Gates hired notable Prairie School architects, among them Frank Lloyd Wright. Fritz Albert, the designer of the Art Institute's piece (right), was best known for sinuous Art Nouveau–influenced vases that demonstrate his expertise as a sculptor, revealed here in the gracefully spiraling leaves and complex mixture of closed and open space.[5] Gates first advertised this vase in 1905, touting its distinctive form as perfect "for decorative purposes either with or without flowers," and continued to offer it for several years, which attests to its popularity.[6]

In 1904, in keeping with the Arts and Crafts movement's agenda of mental and physical rehabilitation through labor, Herbert J. Hall established handicraft shops at his sanatorium in Marblehead, Massachusetts, for the express purpose of revitalizing "nervously worn out patients for the blessing and privilege of quiet manual work."[7] The following year, he hired professional ceramist Arthur E. Baggs to direct the studio. Baggs turned the operation into a commercial and critical success; within a few years, reviewers hailed Marblehead Pottery's conventionalized motifs and harmonizing glazes as pleasing in their "simplicity of form and design."[8] The museum's vase (center), is one of Marblehead's most historically important and complex creations. Annie E. Aldrich's striking frieze of trees and haystacks set against the low horizon of a marsh references the abstract woodblock prints of Arthur Wesley Dow, who ran a summer school in Ipswich, only eighteen miles from Marblehead. There Dow spread his philosophy of contrasting lights and darks, simple lines, open spaces, and muted colors, elements derived from his study of Japanese art.[9]

BRANDON K. RUUD

The Room No. VI

1948

Eldzier Cortor (American, born 1916)

Oil and gesso on Masonite; 107.3 x 80 cm (42 ¼ x 31 ½ in.)

Signed: *E. Cortor* (lower right)
Inscribed: *"The Room No. VI" / Eldzier Cortor / July, 1948 / oil on gesso / size 31" x 42" / Chicago, IL* (verso)

THROUGH PRIOR ACQUISITION OF FRIENDS OF AMERICAN ART AND MR. AND MRS. CARTER H. HARRISON; THROUGH PRIOR GIFT OF THE GEORGE F. HARDING COLLECTION, 2007.329

IN THE 1940s, living conditions for many African Americans on the South Side of Chicago were hard. Racism, segregation, and the increasing pace of migration of blacks from the rural South placed significant pressures on the limited housing stock. Entire families resided together, often in single-room apartments known as kitchenettes.[1] It would not have been unusual for one bed to sleep four people, as Eldzier Cortor depicted in his masterful painting *The Room No. VI*, which he created in Chicago. During the previous decade, he had attended the School of the Art Institute, finding inspiration in the museum's masterpieces of Western painting. He also studied extensively the Field Museum's collection of African art.[2] Although Cortor considered using an abstract idiom, he ultimately decided that, as a black man, it was more important to work in a figurative tradition that could better convey the experiences of African Americans. Synthesizing his various interests, the artist achieved national prominence for his meticulously crafted renderings of black life.[3]

The Room No. VI is one of the finest examples of Cortor's mature painting.[4] Not long after completing the picture, the artist explained that he intended to represent "scenes in the lives of people of the slum areas" and show "the overcrowded condition of people who are obliged to carry out their daily activities of life in the confines of the same four walls in a condition of utmost poverty," while "combin[ing] the figure studies, the bed and the other elements of the room in an interesting pattern."[5] All four figures lying on the bed are cropped by the edges of the painting, creating an almost abstract pattern of interlinking limbs. But the central woman dominates the composition, her form seeming almost upright due to the dramatic bird's-eye perspective. Her elongated appearance reflects the influence of African art; in particular, the sharply defined facial features recall the attenuated treatment found in the art of many of the continent's cultures. Cortor also undoubtedly drew on his knowledge of African sculpture in his depiction of the woman's hair. Although the work has, for the most part, an extraordinarily polished finish, to represent the hair, the artist built up the paint into rough, relieflike elements that interrupt and animate the surface.

Ultimately, Cortor offset the harsh reality of his subject by emphasizing these formal elements of pattern and texture. The brilliant colors and shapes of the bed linens, floorboards, and wallpaper create a dynamic, decorative appearance that alleviates the potential bleakness of the scene. The smooth, lustrous surface—interrupted only by deliberate accretions of paint—further enhances the work's luminous beauty. In *The Room No. VI*, Cortor conveyed the hardships of African American life in Chicago even as he endowed his subjects with profound dignity and grace.

SARAH E. KELLY

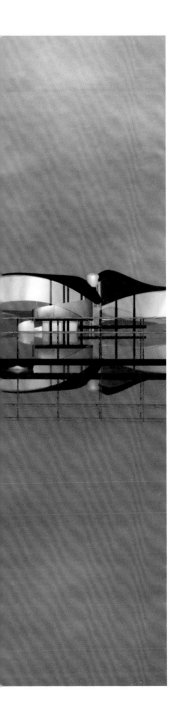

Okavango Delta Spa, Botswana

1997

Roy (founded 2000)
Lindy Roy (South African, born 1963)

Durst Lambda print on paper; 2/5 limited edition, 30.5 x 43.2 cm (12 x 17 in.)

NATIONAL DOCENT SYMPOSIUM FUND, 2009.123.1

THROUGHOUT THE HISTORY of modern architecture, there are rare moments when the strength and vision of a single design establishes a career.[1] Lindy Roy's 1997 proposal for the Okavango Delta Spa in Botswana—illustrated here by a digital print that depicts a gently floating pavilion—is one of those exceptional projects. In many ways, it established her as a leading voice among the new generation of digitally literate architects. Roy's design ideology incorporates influences from disparate spheres, including natural science and technology, to create algorithmic systems that generate architectural works. The resulting plans are simultaneously respectful of context and program, experimental in resolution, and, above all, feasible.[2]

The concept behind the spa, which remains unbuilt, was to merge the world of the sophisticated traveler with the bush experience. The site is truly unique: the world's largest inland delta, the Okavango is the only one to end in a desert and is subject to spectacular seasonal flooding. It is also quite remote, accessible only by helicopter or bush plane. The nature of the landscape made it essential that the freestanding pavilions—or pods—that comprise the spa be merely tethered to the ground rather than set into it with foundation walls. Collectively, the pods evoke the provisional feeling of a temporary settlement. Each unit consists of a low deck with a massage table and chair, a slightly raised area for sleeping, and a fiberglass bathroom unit.

In her proposal, the architect acknowledged local construction techniques and craft traditions. She reconfigured the region's vernacular thatched roofs with steeper slopes to allow for better drainage and then adjusted them to prevailing wind patterns, resulting in an overall shape that is dramatically sculptural in form. Roy also wove translucent fiber-optic strands—similar in diameter to the reeds and straw traditionally used as building materials in Botswana—into guardrails along the spa's walkways. This choice represents a harnessing of new technologies for tactile effects and also demonstrates Roy's abiding interest in fusing systems of construction from different cultures.

It is helpful to think of Roy's approach as algorithmic. This is not to say that her process derives from mathematical equations, but rather that it involves a deliberate series of responses to specific problems, drawing on a range of information to generate cohesive aesthetic solutions. This methodology is best reflected in the spa's overall plan. Below the water level, pipes, pumps, and structural supports allow the complex to function even in extreme flood conditions; above, the design responds to topographical elements, as can be seen in the curvilinear walkways that are secured to abandoned termite mounds. Viewed as an interconnecting system of parts, Roy's spa becomes a conceptual readymade, a work of nomadic architecture that can be resituated anywhere in the delta.

JOSEPH ROSA

New Busan Tower, Busan, South Korea

2002

PATTERNS, Inc. (founded 1999)
Marcelo Spina (Argentine, born 1970)
Georgina Huljich (Argentine, born 1974)

Durst Lambda print on paper, 2/5 limited edition; 61 x 91 cm (24 x 36 in.)

PURCHASED WITH FUNDS PROVIDED BY JANE S. AND HARRY J. HYATT IN HONOR OF KAREN M. HYATT, PRESIDENT
OF THE ARCHITECTURE & DESIGN SOCIETY 2006–2008, 2009.65.1

PROPHETIC UNBUILT DESIGNS can have a profound influence on the next generation of architects. For example, Ludwig Mies van der Rohe's 1922 Glass Skyscraper project, proposed for Berlin, became the model for many emerging voices for decades to follow. However, the evolution of the skyscraper has mostly responded to pragmatic concerns.[1] By the mid-twentieth century, the form had become synonymous with an aesthetic vocabulary of glass and steel built around a central service core. In particular, this core—containing elevators, mechanical systems, plumbing, and stairs—came to define the modernist skyscraper but also limited the height it could achieve.

In their 2002 proposal for New Busan Tower in Busan, South Korea, Marcelo Spina and Georgina Huljich, the principals of the Los Angeles–based studio PATTERNS, Inc., offer a vision of the twenty-first-century skyscraper that departs from these conventions. Emblematic of the work of a new, digitally literate generation of practitioners, their design, illustrated here by a digital print of a rendering, re-envisions the future of such buildings in densely populated cities.[2] Spina and Huljich deconstructed the skyscraper's monolithic central core into separate elements for different functions and then wove them vertically and horizontally into the structural systems where needed. They developed the massing of the tower by making use of the concepts and techniques of aerodynamics. This allows the building to contain enclosed, inhabitable floors as well as open areas through which wind can pass, enabling it to rise higher than traditional examples. While employing a familiar material vocabulary of steel and glass, Spina and Huljich created a building that is composed of solids and voids, all within a structural armature—a design that looks more like a filigreed, monumental form than a conventional skyscraper.[3]

The New Busan Tower is organized into three zones, each with an open-air observatory. The top comprises dining and exhibition space. The middle contains offices for business and governmental activities. The third, at the base of the building, houses restaurants and community facilities such as a theater, as well as public spaces and vehicle parking. In this way, Spina and Huljich decentralize the megastructure's functions just as they break up its core. These decisions allow the design to operate as a city in miniature, an extremely attenuated, reinvented version of an architectural form now over one hundred years old.

JOSEPH ROSA

Cloud Tiles

2009

Designed by Ronan and Erwan Bouroullec Design (founded 1999)
Erwan Bouroullec (French, born 1976)
Ronan Bouroullec (French, born 1971)
Manufactured by Kvadrat (founded 1968), Ebeltoft, Denmark

Wool, Trevira (polyester), rubber, and foam; dimensions variable

GIFT OF KVADRAT, 2009.73

RONAN AND ERWAN BOUROULLEC have been creating work together since founding their studio in 1999 on the outskirts of Paris. Known for their inventive output, the brothers develop designs that are functional yet poetic. They have gained international recognition for their furniture and commercial products, as well as for architectural projects that are based on minimal lines and forms, and imbued with a narrative quality rooted in social and cultural issues. *Sleeping Cabin* (2000), for example, is a white and green metal sleeping loft on stilts. A cross between a bunk bed and a tree house, it was conceived to meet the needs of city dwellers living in cramped quarters. Other Bouroullec projects also question our relationships to space as well as to the ritual activities that make up our daily lives. These include *Modular Kitchen* (1998), a customizable environment for preparing food, and *Joyn Office* (2002), a modular workspace manufactured by Vitra, a Swiss-based pioneer of new types of home and office furnishings.

Further pursuing their exploration of the connections between people and their environments, the brothers have recently developed household accessories and furniture that frame a space, act as room dividers, or simply inject a burst of color and decoration into what might otherwise be bland interiors. Drawing inspiration from forms found in nature, *Algaes*, designed in 2004 for Vitra, are plastic versions of plantlike forms that can be clipped together to create a dense screen reminiscent of algae or seaweed. These *Cloud Tiles*, produced by Kvadrat, a Danish textile company known for its inventive approach to home furnishings, are inherently more structured than *Algaes*, yet are similar in that they, too, provide users with a kit of parts from which they can create a unique arrangement to suit a particular space. The tiles are exceptional for their three-dimensional quality: when joined together, their irregular forms protrude from the wall. Made from wool, these flexible components are held together with an elemental, easy-to-use system of black rubber bands that are not only a functional but also an aesthetic element: visible from the front, they delineate the individual tiles, enhancing their sculptural appearance. Like much of the Bouroullecs' work, *Cloud Tiles* are designed to serve the user. Their distinctive design commands a space but does not disturb the atmosphere of the preexisting architectural environment.

ZOË RYAN

De La Warr Pavilion Chair

2006

Designed by BarberOsgerby (founded 1996)
Edward Barber (British, born 1969)
Jay Osgerby (British, born 1969)
Manufactured by Established & Sons (founded 2004),
London

Cast and pressed aluminum, steel, and nylon; 78 x 58.5 x
56.6 cm (30.7 x 23 x 22.2 in.)

GIFT OF ESTABLISHED & SONS. OBJ. 196172

EDWARD BARBER AND JAY OSGERBY met at the Royal College of Art in London. They founded their studio soon after graduating in 1996 and have since developed a significant body of work acclaimed for its inventive approach to materials and manufacturing methods, and recognized as innovative formal explorations that prompt us to reexamine the objects that we use on a daily basis. Although the team nods to the skilled workmanship of the Arts and Crafts movement, their designs are often highly engineered. Utilizing advanced technological processes and experimenting with materials, they undertake inventive formal and functional analyses that result in elegant, pared-down pieces that respond to human needs. The refined outcome of much of their work often belies the complexity of the development process behind it. For them, a design that combines the appropriate materials and production methods is not the result of a search for the new, but the consequence of striving to create something in the most logical way possible.

Often taking inspiration from marine and aerospace engineering, the pair's approach is nevertheless pragmatic. Yet their interest in using materials and manufacturing techniques in unexpected ways, as a means of reawakening viewers' interest in everyday things, has much in common with the methods of Italian designer Achille Castiglioni. With his brother Pier Giacomo, Castiglione designed such infamous works as the *Toio Lamp* (1962), which consisted of a 300-watt car headlight on a stand made from fishing rod parts, supported by a transformer at the base. The British team shares with their Italian precursors an affinity for creating elegant objects whose beauty lies in their usefulness.

Barber and Osgerby's *De La Warr Pavilion Chair* was created for the restaurants and cafes of the recently restored modernist building designed in 1935 by Erich Mendelsohn and Serge Chermayeff in Bexhill-on-Sea, on the south coast of England. Called upon to replace the original wooden chairs by Alvar Aalto, which had fallen into disrepair, Barber and Osgerby conceived a new design that would be suitable for use throughout the space, including the outdoor terraces. The chair's frame has a sculptural quality reminiscent of the gently curved forms of Aalto's furniture as well as the clean lines of the pavilion itself. Made from aluminum, the soft-edged seat and back are perforated with holes that are both decorative and functional, preventing rain from collecting in the seat and allowing the strong coastal wind to pass through. However, it is the sturdy kick-back leg that differentiates the design from historical versions of four-legged metal dining chairs by modern masters such as Hans Coray. Intellectually rigorous and expertly engineered, this chair attests to the pleasure Barber and Osgerby take in reinterpreting historical forms and approaches to create works that speak to the present.

ZOË RYAN

One Laptop per Child (OLPC) XO Laptop

2007

Conceived and engineered by Nicholas Negroponte (American, born 1943)
Designed by fuseproject (founded 1999)
Yves Béhar (Swiss, born 1967)
Bret Recor (American, born 1974)
Manufactured by Quanta Computer (founded 1988), Taiwan

Medical grade plastic; 24.2 x 22.8 x 3.2 cm (9.5 x 9 x 1.3 in.)

GIFT OF YVES BÉHAR/FUSEPROJECT. 2009.121

NICHOLAS NEGROPONTE, internationally recognized as a pioneer in the field of computer-aided design, is the founder and chairman of One Laptop per Child, a nonprofit organization with the mission of empowering the children of developing countries to learn by providing one connected laptop to every school-age child. In January 2005, he launched his plan for a new, inexpensive laptop computer that would be created specifically for use by children and distributed around the world.

Negroponte teamed with Yves Béhar, a San Francisco–based designer whose studio, fuseproject, is known for innovative commercial products, furniture, and interiors that rethink conventional notions of form and function. Whether designing rubber shoes for Birkenstock, lighting for Herman Miller and Swarovski, accessories for the Mini Cooper, or a line of electronics for Toshiba, Béhar is grounded by his desire to fundamentally improve the quality of everyday life and

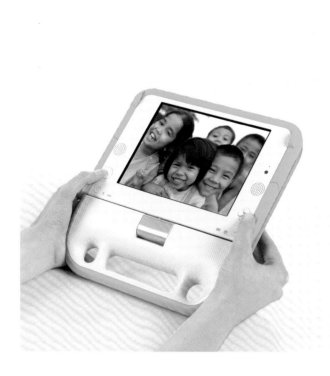

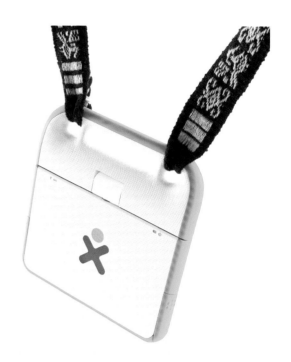

enhance our understanding of the world around us through the objects and spaces that define our environments. Never paying mere lip service to this premise, however, he strives to embed it within his projects in meaningful ways that prompt discussion and ultimately stimulate environmental, political, and social change.

Launched in 2007, the *XO Laptop* fulfills the objective that Negroponte set out: it is technologically sophisticated; it exists as a low-cost alternative to traditional computers; and its compact, lightweight design makes it easily transportable. The screen, which flips and pivots, maximizes functionality and allows children to share information and work communally. The device is further enhanced by the inclusion of antenna ears that, when raised, increase its ability to connect to the Internet over a WiFi network. When flipped down, they shield the USB ports from dust and debris. These features are all protected by a tough plastic shell encased in a rubber edge that ensures

that the laptop is suitable for use in all countries, whatever their climate. As the machine is designed to run on minimal power, a variety of alternative battery-charging methods are being explored so that it can be used in areas of the world with little or no access to electricity. This groundbreaking project, which was named Brit Insurance Design of the Year in 2008 by the London Design Museum, illustrates the power of collaborative design processes. To date, more than one million laptops have been distributed worldwide. Plans are currently underway for a next-generation XO model that will be even more cost effective and consume less power. In this way, One Laptop per Child hopes to more successfully fulfill its goal of providing children in all parts of the world with access to computerized educational tools.

ZOË RYAN

Ordos 100, Lot 006, Inner Mongolia, China

2008

MOS (founded 2003)
Michael Meredith (American, born 1971)
Hilary Sample (American, born 1971)

Digital video, 1/10 limited edition; 5 min. loop

CELIA AND DAVID HILLIARD FUND, 2009.66

WHEN ARCHITECTS PRESENT a design proposal to their clients or the general public, they usually communicate their concept through drawings or scale models. Michael Meredith and Hilary Sample, principals of the studio MOS, have taken the latter medium and combined it with another—video—to add a new element to the lexicon of architectural representation. The result, entitled *Ordos 100*, depicts a house commissioned for a site in Inner Mongolia. Meredith and Sample produced a conventional, handmade cardboard model of the home and made it the subject of their film.

Usually, the most difficult aspect of proposing a design is showing what the building might be like to experience. Meredith and Sample overcame this challenge by presenting a fictional narrative that provides a glimpse of life in the house and showcases the aesthetic intention of their design. The five-minute video shows just two views of the model from dawn to night. As time passes and the scene fades from twilight to darkness, the structure's windows and skylights are intermittently illuminated. The closed captioning that appears at the bottom of the screen narrates a day in the life of a fictional couple identified as X and Y. During the course of the video, a neighbor, Z, who lives in the same development, comes over to socialize and talk about politics. This method of representation allows the narrative of the design to reflect the activities of the occupants. For example, at one point the caption reads, "X goes off to the pool to do some laps," and this is followed by the illumination of windows and a skylight in one portion of the building. Thus, the movements of the individuals within the house are mapped, identifying spaces within the larger structure and revealing that it resembles a small village more than a large home. The soundtrack—generic piano music that has been digitally reversed—sounds like the eccentric work of the modernist composer Erik Satie, adding another level of meaning.

The design of the house reflects the progressive, elegant modern aesthetic for which Meredith and Sample have become known.[1] Its overall massing is composed of interpretations of shapes in traditional Chinese courtyard houses and nomadic yurts. These forms are connected at their corners and together produce numerous open-air spaces. The proportions of each hip-roofed structure vary: the master bedroom has a smaller floor plan and a taller roof than the living room, which has more square footage and a lower ceiling. All the parts of the building have skylights that can be opened to allow air and natural light to circulate.

JOSEPH ROSA

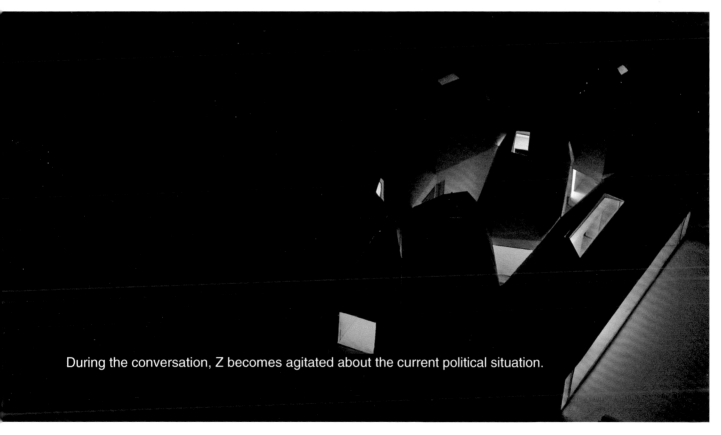

During the conversation, Z becomes agitated about the current political situation.

Wine Flask (Hu)

China

Western Zhou dynasty (c. 1050–771 B.C.), late 10th/early 9th century B.C.

Bronze; 48.5 x 30 x 24.5 cm. (19 ¼ x 11 ¾ x 9 ⅝ in.)

GIFT OF FRED EYCHANER AND TOMMY YANG GUO, 2008.702

THIS HANDSOME FLASK was designed to contain wine during feasts of ancestor worship conducted by the aristocracy of Bronze Age China.[1] An impressive array of bronze vessels used for heating, pouring, carrying, diluting, and drinking wine has been unearthed from tombs and other ritual sites that date between the thirteenth and mid-eleventh centuries B.C., toward the end of China's earliest historical dynasty, the Shang. These objects attest to the prominence of alcohol, which worshippers offered to the deceased and clearly consumed themselves. However, within the subsequent one hundred years, midway through the Western Zhou dynasty, changes in religious belief and practice diminished wine's ceremonial role, and only bronze vessels of the type shown here continued to be made.[2] Excavations of tombs and hastily buried hoards indicate that these gracefully robust flasks, inspired by wider-bodied buckets, were typically cast in matching pairs as part of standardized ritual sets that included additional vessels for grain, meat, and water.

Displaying a masterful integration of silhouette and surface decoration, this example rises from its splayed, ring-shaped foot to a flattened, elliptical body that tapers smoothly to the neck and subtly flares at the rim. Bladelike motifs containing quills encircle the mouth, and hooked scrolls embellish the foot. Two small handles projecting from the neck take the form of fantastic animal heads with long curved snouts and short upturned ears. Simulated strapwork, accented by triangular and diamond-shaped studs, crisscrosses the body, dividing the front and back into quadrants that align with the decorated portions of the neck. Filling each of these areas are heraldic, extravagantly plumed birds that appear in flat, ribbonlike relief against a background of fine spirals. The creatures share protruding eyeballs, hooked beaks, and long, rhythmically curved and spiked crests, wings, and tail feathers. The central pair confronts each other head-to-head, while those around the neck and those across the lower belly are shown back-to-back. The last are the largest, boldest, and most intricately detailed.[3]

This flask was most likely fitted with a lid and had flat rings suspended from the handles. Inscriptions cast in comparable Western Zhou vessels indicate that it was likely an heirloom buried for safekeeping rather than a grave good that would have been interred with its original owner.[4] At some point after it was discovered, the flask was cleaned of its natural patination; coated with a mixture of clay, pigment, and organic material; and darkened, probably by heating. The resulting smooth, blackish-brown surface is distinctive to many ancient bronzes collected in the late nineteenth and early twentieth centuries.[5]

ELINOR PEARLSTEIN

Coin with Portraits of Cleopatra and Mark Antony

C. 36 B.C.

Greco-Roman, minted in the eastern Mediterranean region

Silver tetradrachm; diam. 2.6 cm (1 ¹⁄₁₆ in.), 15.22 g

Inscribed: *ΚΛΕΟΠΑΤΡΑ ΘΕΑ ΝΕΩΤΕΡΑ* (the younger goddess Cleopatra; obverse); *ΑΝΤΩΟΝΟC ΑΥΤΟΚΡΑΤΩΡ ΤΡΙΤΟΝ ΤΡΙΩΝ ΑΝΔΡΩΝ* (Antony, imperator, third of the triumvirate; reverse)

KATHERINE K. ADLER MEMORIAL FUND, 2008.173

THIS RARE AND exquisite silver coin portrays two of the most famous figures of antiquity, the charismatic Egyptian queen Cleopatra and the ambitious Roman warlord Mark Antony.[1] Cleopatra ruled Egypt during the period when Rome was expanding its empire eastward toward the territories she controlled. By allying herself politically and personally first with Julius Caesar and, after his death, with Mark Antony, the queen hoped to maintain Egypt's autonomy and expand her own authority. The powerful political alliance between Antony and Cleopatra threatened Caesar's heir, his great-nephew Octavian, who in 33 B.C. defeated their forces in a decisive sea battle at Actium, which led to the pair's suicides.

To pay their armies and satisfy their other debts, Antony and Cleopatra minted coins bearing their likenesses. This example is remarkable in that it depicts both the general and the queen. Antony, seen here at bottom, is framed by an inscription that identifies him as a commander and one of Rome's trio of rulers. He is represented with short hair, a flat nose, a strong chin, and a long, thick neck. Cleopatra, shown at top, has a profile that is startlingly similar to Antony's, right down to the Adam's apple on her massive neck. This similarity was purposeful, since other coins issued by Cleopatra display a distinctly feminine profile. More of her figure is depicted than is Antony's, including her upper torso, which showcases her legendary pearl jewelry. An inscription and a crown circling her carefully braided hair identify her as a queen; she was, in fact, Egypt's last.

Cleopatra appears on the front of the coin, in the place of prestige, and Antony is on the back. This is unusual because, although she was queen of Egypt, her country was a subservient ally of Rome. By pairing their faces on coinage, the rulers advertised a powerful new partnership that put Egypt's enormous agricultural riches at the disposal of one of Rome's rulers. Antony and Cleopatra planned to govern Egypt equally and cooperatively. To the joint venture the queen brought her hereditary right to rule, while Antony brought Roman military power. Their coin relayed this message in its coupling of remarkably similar images and in the inscriptions circling the heads. This kind of bold statement undoubtedly offended their enemies in Rome, especially Octavian, and helped bring about their eventual downfall.

MARY GREUEL

A Scroll from the Jingoji Sutra and Textile Wrapper

12th century

Japan

Hand scroll: gold and silver pigments on indigo-dyed paper; 25.8 cm x 1,289 cm (10 ⅛ in. x 468 ³⁄₁₆ in.)

Wrapper: bamboo, silk, mica, and gilt bronze; 45.5 x 31.1 cm (17 ¹⁵⁄₁₆ x 12 ¼ in.)

PURCHASED WITH FUNDS PROVIDED BY THE WESTON FOUNDATION. 2008.157-58

This textile wrapper would originally have protected ten scrolls. Several such bundles would be contained in a lacquer box.

THIS SCROLL AND wrapper are from a famous edition of sutras, the teachings that constitute Buddhist scripture. The roll belonged to a set of five thousand that was likely commissioned by Emperor Toba of Japan (r. 1107–23) and completed in 1185 during the reign of his son, Emperor Go-Shirakawa (r. 1155–58), when they were dedicated to Jingoji Temple in Kyoto. Of the original scrolls—which contained the entire Buddhist canon—about two thousand remain at the temple. Each wrapper would have contained about ten scrolls, and lacquer boxes would have held several such bundles. Beginning in the nineteenth century, the sutras were sold to pay for the repair and maintenance of the temple complex.

The outside cover features a design of flowers and arabesques, and within that design, a label cartouche states that this scroll contains the Great Collection Sutra chapter 9. The frontispiece (far right), which is the same for all scrolls in the set, shows the Buddha preaching at Vulture Peak. Here, in Madhya Pradesh, India, he is said to have shared his best-known teachings with a gathered assembly of thousands, including bodhisattvas and monks. The line drawings of the figures were made with gold pigment, which the artist applied in confident, precise strokes of the pen. At the beginning of the text portion, the seal of the temple appears in red. The ruled lines of text were rendered in silver and the Chinese characters themselves were brushed in gold in a balanced and orderly script. The textile wrapper (left) is composed of dyed bamboo that was fastened together with colorful threads, laid upon a sheet of mica backed with paper, and then framed in silk brocade. The metal fixtures take the shape of butterflies.

Making luxurious editions of sutras was seen as an act of faith, even more so if they included the entire Buddhist canon. Those with the means to launch such projects believed that all involved—especially the main patron—would receive great spiritual benefits. Therefore, decorated sutras were some of the most extravagant artistic commissions of their time, reaching their height of popularity during the eleventh and twelfth centuries.

JANICE KATZ

大集經月藏分第十二分布閻浮提品第七

尒時世尊既知一切諸來大眾於三寶所皆
生深信尊敬仰得未曾有更不信事諸餘

天已告他化自在天王樂天王兜率陁天

王須夜摩天王帝釋天王四大天王及諸眷

Four-Armed Dancing God Ganesha with His Rat Mount

16th/17th century

Nepal

Gilt bronze worked in repoussé; 50.9 x 39.9 x 14 cm (20 x 15 ⅝ x 5 ½ in.)

JAMES W. AND MARILYNN ALSDORF COLLECTION, 2008.701

THROUGHOUT NEPAL'S Kathmandu Valley, temple and palace doorways are adorned with highly detailed gilt metal repoussé or wood panel surrounds. They highlight the passage from the material, secular world to the realm of the sacred and spiritual.[1] The Art Institute's gilt bronze repoussé plaque depicts the Hindu deity Ganesha, the elephant-headed god who is invoked as the Remover of Obstacles and the Lord of New Beginnings. In Nepal, he is sometimes a doorway guardian, a particularly appropriate function given that he often plays a liminal role in Hindu mythology: Ganesha not only protects literal entrances but also presides over the thresholds that are to be crossed in order to start something new. There are many temples dedicated to this god in the Kathmandu Valley.[2]

While usually shown as a pot-bellied boy, the deity appears here as a graceful, slender youth dancing with his legs bent to the sides as he gently nudges his tiny rat mount. His pose is one of several that characterize the god Shiva, who is both his father and Lord of the Dance. In his hands, Ganesha holds his typical attributes: a battle axe, a bowl of *laddu* (sticky, ball-shaped sweets), and a lotus blossom with a stem. Characteristics of the Nepalese style include the god's adornments: he wears a tripartite crown upon flowing sausage-roll locks, prominent diamond-shaped earrings, and fluttering sashes. The hairstyle in particular displays a stylistic link to the art of India's Gupta period, which lasted from the fourth to sixth centuries.[3] This was India's classical age, the period immediately following the appearance of the earliest images of the god.

There are many myths offering different explanations of how Ganesha obtained his elephant head. According to one, his mother Parvati, the consort of Shiva, gave birth to a beautiful boy by rubbing the dust off her body. She then instructed the child to guard her door while she bathed. Shiva arrived and tried to enter, but the boy blocked the way. In a rage, Shiva knocked off Ganesha's head, sending Parvati into floods of tears. Rushing out into the forest to find a replacement, Shiva cut off the head of the first animal he saw, which happened to be an elephant. Whatever his mythic origins, the beloved Ganesha, as Lord of New Beginnings, is a particularly appropriate symbol for the museum's newly launched Alsdorf Galleries of Indian, Southeast Asian, Himalayan, and Islamic Art.

MADHUVANTI GHOSE

Maharao Guman Singh Riding an Elephant in Procession

1770

India, Rajasthan, Kota

Opaque watercolor, black ink, and gold on tan paper; page: 37.5 x 54 cm (14 ¾ x 21 ¼ in.)

Inscribed: *Commissioned by Maharao Chattar Sal, a portrait of Maharao Guman Singh seated on an elephant and proceeding on a journey* (in Hindi, in Devanagari script, in the top red border); *This is a portrait of Guman Singh, 1770* A.D. (*samvat* 1827) (in Hindi, in Devanagari script, twice on the reverse)

MRS. CLIVE RUNNELLS FUND, 2008.23

THIS MAGNIFICENT PAINTING comes from the princely state of Kota in Rajasthan in the northwest of present-day India. This small kingdom—about ninety miles long from north to south and about eighty miles wide—is renowned for its exceptional paintings of battles, durbars (court scenes), elephant fights, hunts, and royal processions that were made from the seventeenth through nineteenth centuries.

In this dynamic portrait, Maharao Guman Singh (r. 1764–71), ruler of Kota, rides astride a richly caparisoned elephant, outlined against a rounded hill with an orange and gold sky above. The young, energetic mount charges forward with upraised trunk and flying tail. The haloed king, armed with bow, quivers, and a shield, and with his trusty sword tucked in his belt, holds a goad and a crescent-shaped arrow. His retinue, all of whom bear arms, are probably on their way to war. Running ahead, the infantry carry orange sword bags, while lancers and heavily armed cavalry close ranks behind. In 1670 the ruler had to defend his kingdom against the Marathas, marauders from what is now the state of Maharashtra, who were attacking Kota's southern border.[2] The Art Institute's watercolor may depict this campaign.

The maharao was about forty years old when he ascended the throne. He was a great patron of art, as evidenced by an extensive set of over 240 *ragamala* paintings (depictions of musical modes, called ragas) that he commissioned. It is the largest known ragamala set.[3] Apart from the painting shown here, there are few published portraits of the king. This one was commissioned by his brother and predecessor, Maharao Chattar Sal. Guman Singh's reign was cut short as he suffered from ulcers and died, possibly from an application of poisoned bandages, in January 1771.[4]

MADHUVANTI GHOSE

Blue Phoenix

1921

Ōmura Kōyō (Japanese, 1891–1983)

Pair of six-panel screens; ink, color, and gold on silk;
each 190 x 376 cm (74 ¹³⁄₁₆ x 148 in.)

PRESIDENT'S EXHIBITION AND ACQUISITION FUND; ALSDORF
DISCRETIONARY FUND; RUSSELL TYSON ENDOWMENT FUND; PURCHASED
WITH FUNDS PROVIDED BY THE WESTON FOUNDATION, 2007.359.1–2

THIS PAIR OF SCREENS by Ōmura Kōyō envelop the viewer in a close-up depiction of a lush tropical forest inhabited by birds of many sizes, most notably a type of exotic pheasant, which the artist calleded the "Blue Phoenix." In the right screen, a pair of birds perch calmly. By contrast, in the screen at left, an active male engages in a mating display, fanning out his patterned feathers across the panels. The dynamic composition fills every inch of the oversized screens, and the bright greens and reds of the foliage are set off by the subtle glow of the silk ground, which was backed in luminous gold foil.

This subject matter comes from sketches Ōmura did during a long trip to the Dutch East Indies, now Indonesia. The flowering plant is the Royal Poinciana, which produces large colorful blossoms. Known variously as the Flamboyant Tree, Peacock Flower, Flame of the Forest, or Flame Tree, it is native to Madagascar, but also present in Jakarta's parks and its Ragunan Zoo, where Ōmura likely encountered it. The pheasants, which are known as the Great Argus, are native to

Borneo and Sumatra. They are extremely shy, so it is probable that Ōmura observed them in a zoo. This hypothesis is supported by the presence on the right side of the left screen of an Alexandrine parakeet, a species not native to Indonesia.[1]

The artist was a star of his generation. Born in Fukuyama, whose city art museum holds many of his works, he graduated from the Kyoto Municipal School of Painting in 1914 and became the pupil of Takeuchi Seiho, a renowned master of Nihonga, or traditional Japanese painting. From 1912 until World War II, Ōmura showed regularly at Japan's premier exhibitions. He also displayed his work to admiring audiences in France and Germany, gaining an international popularity that was rare for Japanese artists at the time.

These works are without a doubt the masterpiece of Ōmura's career. However, they were exhibited only once prior to their acquisition by the Art Institute: at the Third Teiten (Teikoku bijutsuin tenrankai; Exhibition of the Imperial Academy of Fine Arts, Tokyo) in 1921. One contemporary critic remarked, "The vivid colors of the tropical birds, overflowing with vigor, cause deep satisfaction within the viewer—a sensation similar to that of reading greatly solemn sutra texts from the time in ancient India when many sages lived; I feel that we have now reached a similar moment in our history."[2] The screens proved so popular that subsequent exhibitions of the artist's work invariably included preparatory sketches, alternate smaller versions, or photographs of them.

JANICE KATZ

Tableau Vert

1952

Ellsworth Kelly (American, born 1923)

Oil on wood; 74.3 x 99.7 cm (29 ¼ x 39 ¼ in.)

GIFT OF THE ARTIST, 2009.51

ELLSWORTH KELLY'S WORK emphasizes pure color, form, and line, yet his abstraction is rooted in close observation of environments both natural and manmade. Inspired by a brief visit to Paris during World War II, he made the city his home from 1948 to 1954 with the support of the G. I. Bill. This distance from the New York art world—and most notably from its dominant style, Abstract Expressionism—freed the artist to create reductive compositions that were at times inflected by chance processes such as automatic drawing and a collage technique in which he tore up old drawings, scattered the pieces, and affixed them where they landed on the page.[1] Reflecting on this period, Kelly remarked, "I did not want to 'invent' pictures, so my sources were in nature, which to me includes everything seen."[2] Translating his observations into pure color, he began to experiment with the possibilities of multipanel painting—specifically, joined, identically scaled monochromes that were each painted to the very edge of the canvas.

In 1952, while staying outside Paris, Kelly discovered a book on Claude Monet and wrote to the artist's stepson, Jean-Pierre Hoschedé, who resided in Giverny, the small village in Normandy where the Impressionist had lived and worked for over forty years. During the ensuing visit, as Kelly recalled:

[Hoschedé] took us out to the big studio where all the paintings of water lilies were kept. There must have been at least a dozen huge paintings, each on two easels. There were birds flying around. The paintings had been abandoned, really . . . And then we went into a second studio, and there must have been a hundred paintings there of medium size that were just jammed together . . . I liked the quality of the painting. Monet was losing his sight and was fascinated by the movement of leaves underwater.[3]

Influenced by these works, the artist made *Tableau Vert*, his first single-canvas monochrome.[4] Displaying subtle, mottled brushwork—a rarity in Kelly's oeuvre—the picture was created by mixing thin, transparent layers of blue and green pigments to achieve the quality of "grass moving under water."[5] The nuanced shifts in tone and value seem to reference Monet's studies of light. This vibrant painting not only shows the Impressionist's influence on the young Kelly but also represents the formative years of his training. *Tableau Vert* is thus both a fitting complement to the Art Institute's peerless Monet holdings and an important addition to its rich collection of Kelly's work.

JENNY GHEITH

Da Creepy Lady

1970

Jim Nutt (American, born 1938)

Acrylic on Plexiglas, enamel on wood frame; 191.5 x 130.8 cm
(75 ³/₈ x 51 ¹/₂ in)

PROMISED GIFT OF THE HENRY AND GILDA BUCHBINDER FAMILY
COLLECTION, 21.2009

JIM NUTT WAS a member of the Hairy Who, an irreverent, loose affiliation of Chicago artists who exhibited together at the Hyde Park Art Center from 1966 to 1968 and whose work shared similar stylistic inclinations—a focus on the figure, an emphasis on distortion, and the use of garish colors and pop-culture quotations. Influenced by the aesthetics of advertisements, cinema, comic books, folk art, Surrealism, and tribal art, Nutt's darkly humorous and sometimes violent creations present an emphatically vernacular, unconventionally sensuous, and often explicitly sexual vision of the human figure, the principal theme of his art.[1]

Nutt first became well known for painting on the back of Plexiglas to create pictures with a seamless, glossy finish that he called a "super surface."[2] The artist made *Da Creepy Lady*, a monumental example of this meticulous and painstakingly slow technique, right before he stopped working in this manner.[3] At the center of the painting is a confrontation between a man and woman, a common subject for Nutt. Clad only in undergarments and high heels, the large female figure narrows her eyes at her opponent, who is shown from the chest up, sticking his tongue out at her. A potent figure, she bears sharp claws on her right hand in place of fingernails; her left appears deformed. Her lips are green, and her face is patterned with red spots that recall those of a wild animal, echoing the similarly decorated frame. Responding to criticisms that his depictions of women at this time were vulgar, Nutt explained, "First of all, I don't know what you mean by 'vulgar.' My women are dream women. I can look at, say, a magazine ad about varicose veins—you know, the 'before and after' kind—and I think it's an exciting image. I really like it. It's like a Max Ernst collage, like from the *One Hundred Headed Woman*. That's what I try to do."[4]

Da Creepy Lady's battle of the sexes is coupled with unnerving ancillary images that surround the main figures. These small narrative bursts include a torso dotted with fingernails; a small scene of a skyscraper with an airplane overhead; a pimple-covered chest; a ladder; and a woman with an unidentified, clearly invasive form sticking out from beneath her skirt. These exaggerated and at times grotesque motifs, combined with the color contrasts and linear emphasis of Nutt's graphic style, create a masterful example of the Hairy Who's raucous visual language. Commenting on this period in his career, Nutt stated that in his pictures he sought "ways of breaking down a static situation."[5] This approach is evident in the monumental scale and abundant use of supporting scenes throughout *Da Creepy Lady*—all of which perfectly express the fantastically charged, animated feel of Nutt's early work.

JENNY GHEITH

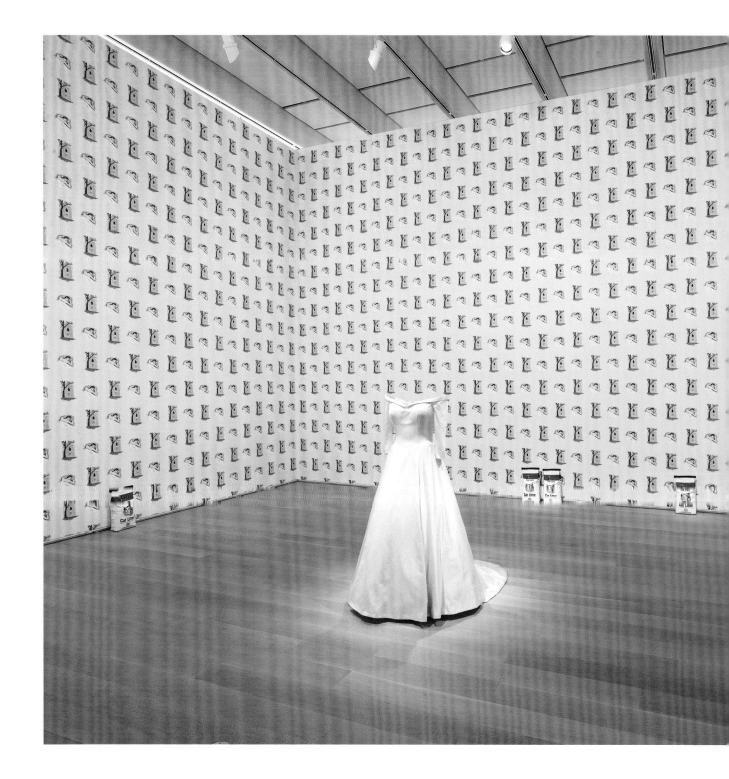

Untitled

1989-96

Robert Gober (American, born 1954)

Silk satin, muslin, linen, tulle, welded steel, hand-printed silkscreen on paper, cast hydro-stone plaster, vinyl acrylic paint, ink, and graphite; dimensions variable

RESTRICTED GIFT OF STEFAN T. EDLIS AND H. GAEL NEESON FOUNDATION; THROUGH PRIOR GIFTS OF MR. AND MRS. JOEL STARRELS AND FOWLER MCCORMICK, 2008.174

ROBERT GOBER'S INSISTENTLY handmade, deceptively complex sculptures are re-creations of familiar things. As imitations, his works have an uncanny, disquieting effect. In 1989, at the Paula Cooper Gallery in New York, the artist constructed two three-sided rooms defined by temporary sheetrock walls. The installation shown here was the first room of that exhibition. Outfitted with wallpaper that alternated images of a sleeping white man and a lynched black man hanging from a tree, the space was lined with eight hand-painted plaster reproductions of bags of cat litter.[1] At the center was an empty wedding dress on a welded steel armature. The exhibition, a dystopic meditation on gender, race, sexuality, and the violence of contemporary American life, was a watershed in the history of recent art. In many ways, it can be understood retrospectively as having announced the end of the excesses of the 1980s, inaugurating the coolly critical, identity-based art of the 1990s.

In 2009 Gober reflected on this piece prior to its installation in the Modern Wing:

> The painful imagery . . . was meant as a reminder of fact—the ugly and unforgettable reality of the United States' history. By putting this image onto endlessly repeating wallpaper, I made an attempt to say, metaphorically, that this was not an isolated event and that in ways it has become our background. The sculpture of the empty wedding dress is a vase waiting to be filled. It represents the supposed white purity that often triggered or justified the violence depicted on the walls. It also represents a vessel that is ready to be filled with all of the optimistic hopes and dreams of marriage. And to many Americans, gay Americans (an estimated 10 percent of our population), it is a reminder of equality denied. The sculptures of bags of cat litter are the link between the violent imagery and the wedding dress, the metaphorical fulcrum. Cat litter both absorbs the stench of excrement (the wallpaper) and it allows for domestic intimacy (think diapers). It is also a reminder of the sacred vows that those who wear the dress profess—to care for the body of your loved ones "in sickness and in health, till death do us part."[2]

Like his other works, Gober's installation articulates the deeply idiosyncratic archaeology of his own imagination, memories, and experiences as well as of shared concerns drawn from everyday social exigencies. As the artist's comments about gay marriage suggest, time has transformed—and will continue to change—the meaning of this highly personal yet broadly critical social statement, which remains as challenging and poignant today as it was twenty years ago.

JAMES RONDEAU

Vignette Suite

2005–08

Kerry James Marshall (American, born 1955)

Suite of five paintings; *Vignette 2* (2005): acrylic on Plexiglas; *Vignette 2.25* (2008), *Vignette 2.50* (2008), and *Vignette 2.75* (2008): acrylic on polyvinyl; *Vignette 3* (2005): acrylic on Plexiglas; 186 × 155 cm (73 1/4 × 61 in.) each

THROUGH PRIOR GIFT OF ADELINE YATES; BENJAMIN ARGILE MEMORIAL, CYRUS HALL McCORMICK, ALFRED AND MAY TIFFENBRONNER MEMORIAL, MR. AND MRS. FRANK G. LOGAN PRIZE, PAULINE PALMER PRIZE, BROADUS JAMES CLARKE MEMORIAL, NORMAN WAIT HARRIS PRIZE, WILLIAM H. BARTELS PRIZE, JOYCE VAN PILSUM, LAURA T. MAGNUSON ACQUISITION, ANN M. VIELEHR PRIZE, AND ADA S. GARRETT PRIZE FUNDS; FLORA MAYER WITKOWSKY AWARD FOR AMERICAN ART; BOLES C. AND HYACINTH G. DRECHNEY, AND MR. AND MRS. J. F. BROWER PRIZE FUNDS; THE MUNICIPAL ART LEAGUE PRIZE FOR PORTRAITURE; MARJORIE AND LOUIS SUSMAN, MARTIN B. CAHN PRIZE, AND ELISABETH MATHEWS FUNDS, 2008.481–5

KERRY JAMES MARSHALL'S paintings, drawings, and installations examine the representation of African American popular and historical culture. Grounded in the tradition of history painting, his works employ art-historical themes and references as a way of recontextualizing African American issues. *Vignette Suite* (right) developed out of Marshall's interest in initiating a "Black Rococo" aesthetic that uses this luxuriant, visually excessive style to depict the lives of black men and women, instead of the upper class of France's ancien regime.[1] In this suite of five paintings, Marshall uses the vignette, a decorative design that focuses on a specific moment from a narrative and is framed by asymmetrical, amorphously shaded borders.[2] Here, however, he turned these typically small ornamental motifs into grand scenes.

According to the artist, the series' portrayal of a woman in fluid aerial motion responds to Jean-Honoré Fragonard's painting *The Swing* (1766; Wallace Collection, London). In *Vignette 2.5*, a scene of delicately veiled eroticism and vulgarity, the viewer can gaze directly up the woman's dress, mirroring Fragonard's composition. Rococo figures were meant to look light, but here the couple is awkwardly posed and heavy. Somewhat comically, the man struggles to keep his partner in the air; in *Vignette 2.25* (far right), she seems capable of knocking him down. Classical statuary or ancient ruins are usually embedded in Rococo landscapes, and Marshall acknowledges this convention as well, filling the scenery with symbols of the African American past and present. While *Vignettes 2* and *3* show African masks and ceramics, *Vignettes 2.25* and *2.75* include symbols of African American political activism and resistance such as a black panther (a reference to the radical group of the same name), a Black Power fist, an Egyptian pyramid, the finials on top of the Black Liberation flag, fists breaking through chains, an image of the African continent, and the star and crescent of Islam. In the background of *Vignette 2* appears a Modernist building whose placement serves as a gentle reminder of the complicated relationship between Modernism and African art.

Vignette Suite is Marshall's only set of paintings designed as a cycle and intended to form a single installation.[3] Taken as a whole, this ambitious suite captures the artist's multifaceted, ever-evolving approach to the representation of African American identity. In Marshall's words, "From one side you got the struggle from the other side you get the aspiration."[4]

JENNY GHEITH

Installation views of *Vignette Suite* in the Modern Wing. In the image at top, from left to right, appear *Vignette 2.25* and *Vignette 2*. At bottom, from left to right, are *Vignette 3*, *Vignette 2.75*, and *Vignette 2.5*.

Hinoki

2007

Charles Ray (American, born 1953)

Cypress; 170.2 x 762 x 579.1 cm (67 x 300 x 228 in.), installed

THROUGH PRIOR GIFTS OF MARY AND LEIGH BLOCK, MR. AND MRS. JOEL STARRELS, MRS. GILBERT W. CHAPMAN, AND MR. AND MRS. ROY J. FRIEDMAN; RESTRICTED GIFT OF DONNA AND HOWARD STONE, 2007.771

THE WORK OF CHICAGO-BORN sculptor Charles Ray is based on a complex interplay between realism and artifice. Possessed by the idea of making a sculpture of a fallen tree, he spent several years searching for the perfect model. In 1998, while walking in the woods of central California, Ray encountered a coastal oak that had lain on the forest floor for decades. The artist was drawn to the complexity of the tree's surfaces; over time, gravity, weather, insects, and the sun's rays had done considerable damage, and the trunk was partially sunk into the ground. Ray reflected,

> At one point, I determined that its armature could be its *pneuma*, the Greek word for *breath*, *wind*, or *life* . . . It then struck me that the breath or life of the sculpture could be manifested in the very act of sculpting. Making a wood carving of the log by starting from the inside and working my way out would bring a trajectory of life and intentionality to this great fallen tree.[1]

Aided by several assistants, Ray cut the tree apart with a chainsaw and transported it to his Los Angeles studio. Silicone molds were taken, and from them, a fiberglass version of the log was produced. This form was then cut into five sections and sent to Osaka, Japan, where, for over four years, master carvers led by Yuboku Mukoyoshi worked by eye from the model, painstakingly rendering an actual-size replica out of Japanese cypress, or *hinoki*. The artist was attracted to this specific wood for many reasons, among them that it is the material of choice for traditional Japanese carvings of the Buddha, which are made for both public temples and private devotional purposes. Ray reports that he was also "drawn to the woodworkers because of their tradition of copying work that is beyond restoration. In Japan, when an old temple or Buddha can no longer be maintained, it is remade."[2]

Every inch of the work's creased, creviced, and gnarled surface—both inside and outside the hollow trunk—is incised with a dense network of tiny, overlapping, fractal-like marks. The most minute attributes of the original tree's surface are faithfully rendered, including worm holes, termite trails, and even the marks of the chainsaw used to dismantle it. By employing pristine, sturdy wood to create a sculpture of an already partially collapsed and rotted oak, Ray both re-created the fallen tree and extended its existence.[3] Inevitably, however, *Hinoki* will change over time: its patina will darken, it will begin to rot, and, in hundreds of years, it will eventually decay—just like the oak tree that inspired it, albeit more slowly.

JAMES RONDEAU AND JENNY GHEITH

The Whitfield Cup

1590

London, England

Made by John Spilman (English, born Germany, died 1626)

Gilt silver and ostrich egg; h. 32 cm (12 ½ in.) with cover

THE MARY SWISSLER OLDBERG MEMORIAL FUND, 2009.113

IN THE SIXTEENTH century, Europe witnessed the rise of an urban upper-middle class whose wealth did not derive from the church or the monarchy but rather from banking, law, manufacturing, and trade. For these newly empowered people—including the Whitfields, successful lawyers with courtly connections—works of art symbolized prosperity, social status, and sophistication. Accordingly, such objects led relatively sheltered lives and were kept on display to impress visitors. The elaborately chased, embossed, and engraved Whitfield Cup (far right) is an exceptional example of this kind of piece.

In the 1500s, ostrich eggs were called "gripes eggs" as they were then thought to be laid by the mythical beast, the griffin. In the 1574 inventory of the contents of the royal Jewel House in the Tower of London, a list of hundreds of silver and gold items included only three objects incorporating ostrich eggs, which attests to the rarity of such exotic creations at the time. The Whitfield Cup is even more closely associated with royalty since it bears the hallmark of Elizabeth I's jeweler, John Spilman, a Bavarian-trained goldsmith who immigrated to London and registered his hallmark there in 1582. In fact, the piece may have been commissioned in 1590 by the Virgin Queen herself. At the bottom of the egg's interior, where it joins the stem, Spilman inserted a conspicuous Tudor rose, the emblem reserved for Elizabeth's use, and which originally would have been even more visible because it was decorated in blue, red, and white enamels, now missing. Although the exact circumstances of the cup's production and early existence remain to be determined, family tradition suggests that it may have been presented to John Whitfield by the queen. When Whitfield's grandson—also John Whitfield—drew up a lengthy will in 1687, he specifically listed several heirlooms, including "the Estrich [*sic*] Cup and Queen Elizabeth's Glass which was my grandfathers."[1]

Presumably, it is this John Whitfield who commissioned the Dutch artist Pieter Gerritsz von Roestraeten to paint *Still Life with Ostrich Egg Cup and the Whitfield Heirlooms* (below). It is extremely unusual to be able to match the painted images in a still life with the actual objects they depict. Many of the other items in the painting also seem to be mentioned in the 1687 will, including "a large medal of Arabian gold, of about 10 pounds in value and his mother's locket of diamonds in three parts, also a large medal of the king of Sweden . . . his Grandfathers sealed Ring, and my Striking Watch."[2]

At present, it is not known when the painting and cup parted ways. They were reunited by the last private owner of the cup, Lord Harris of Peckham, in the 1990s. When his collection was sold in 2008, the pieces were offered together and acquired by the Art Institute.[3]

CHRISTOPHER MONKHOUSE

Pieter Gerritsz von Roestraeten (Dutch, 1630–1700). *Still Life with Ostrich Egg Cup and the Whitfield Heirlooms*, c. 1670. Oil on canvas; 65.4 x 75.6 cm (25 ¾ x 29 ¾ in.). European Decorative Arts Purchase Fund, 2009.114.

Side Chair

c. 1802–10

London, England

After a design by Thomas Hope (1769–1831)

Mahogany, ebony, and beech, with new leather upholstery on seat; 87 x 64 x 72 cm (34.2 x 25.2 x 28.3 in.)

ROBERT ALLERTON PURCHASE FUND, MARY WALLER LANGHORNE MEMORIAL FUND, JOHN AND NEVILLE BRYAN FUND, 2009.127

WHEN THOMAS CHIPPENDALE published *Gentleman and Cabinetmaker's Director* in 1754, his name almost immediately became synonymous with the Rococo style. Similarly, in 1807, when Thomas Hope issued his *Household Furniture and Interior Decoration*, his name attached itself forever to the Neoclassical. But while Chippendale was a practicing cabinetmaker whose illustrations depicted pieces that could actually be ordered from his shop, Hope was a connoisseur and collector from a wealthy banking family who wished to shape taste by commissioning cabinetmakers to produce objects for his London home, pieces that he, more often than not, designed himself. As Hope's house could be visited upon application, it instantly became a mecca for art lovers, from professional architects to informed amateurs. *Household Furniture* was readily available through the commercial publisher Longman and was illustrated by simple outline drawings that could be inexpensively reproduced, forwarding Hope's goal of making his home and its contents accessible to, and available for copying by, as wide an audience as possible. His success can be measured by the huge influence the book enjoyed at the time of its initial publication, as well as during the Empire Revival in the 1890s and more recently in the 1970s, thanks to Postmodernism's reappropriation of historical styles.

Of all the forms illustrated in *Household Furniture*, seating received the most attention, from the saber-legged *klismos*, a relatively conventional Greek-style chair, to the highly individualistic example shown here. Originally conceived as one of a pair, the piece was intended for use in a room containing Classical vases. It exhibits an idiosyncratic profile—due especially to the exaggerated concave and convex shape of the vertical stiles—that might well have been inspired by ancient chairs depicted on the pots that would have sat on the shelves directly above it. The inspiration for the profile of the stiles may also have come from the distinctive boughs of the gondolas that ply Venice's Grand Canal, for the shape is strikingly similar and these boats have attracted the attention of visitors for hundreds of years.

In the second half of the twentieth century, the bold proportions and arresting silhouettes of early-nineteenth-century Neoclassical furniture caught the attention of a number of Postmodern designers and critics, including the Scottish architect James Stirling, who acquired superlative examples of Hope's furniture for his own home, including this chair.[1] The architect was a passionate admirer of this deign. Remarking that "Hope chairs, with their statuesque simplicity and swooping curves, were like individual monuments designed for Regency drawing rooms," he confessed that he was attracted to them because "they are extreme, outrageous, over the top, eccentric, and much more gutsy than anything French Empire. There's absolutely no feeling of restraint or lack of confidence."[2]

CHRISTOPHER MONKHOUSE

Wall Clock

c. 1880

Paris, France
Made by l'Escalier de Cristal (1804–1923)

Bronze, gilt bronze, and cloisonné enamel; 94 x 40.6 x
22.9 cm (37 x 16 x 9 in.)

MARY WALLER LANGHORNE MEMORIAL FUND; HARRIET A. FOX FUND, MR.
AND MRS. E. B. SMITH, JR., 2008.491

THIS BRONZE AND ENAMEL clock originally came
to New York from Paris in about 1880, shortly after it had
been made by the firm l'Escalier de Cristal, which specialized
in producing small luxury items and marketing them to an
international clientele for whom money was no object.[1] The
clock's intended destination was the home—then under
construction on the west side of Fifth Avenue between 51st
and 52nd streets—of the richest man in America, the railroad
magnate William H. Vanderbilt, whose net worth was then
estimated at two hundred million dollars. For this essay in
conspicuous consumption, Vanderbilt turned to Herter
Brothers, America's leading interior decorators. While the
firm provided many of the furnishings from its own extensive
workrooms, it also imported selected works of art from
abroad with the active assistance of Vanderbilt's art advisor,
Samuel Putnam Avery.

In addition to selecting modern masters for his client's
picture gallery, Avery could well have been responsible for
acquiring this clock as a central adornment for one of Herter's
most elaborate and exotic creations, the Japanese Parlor.
Situated strategically between the drawing room and the
dining room, it contrasted with the rest of the interiors, which
were decorated in a Renaissance Revival style. Thus far, the
wall clock appears to be the only object from the parlor that
has survived.

In order that his domestic arrangements would enjoy a
wider audience, Vanderbilt commissioned an elaborately
illustrated four-volume survey of the home and its contents
that appeared in 1883 and 1884. The chapter on the Japanese
Parlor commences with an illustration of the wall clock, as
well as the following description:

> Here all the furniture and decorations are in Japanese taste,
> and as far as may be, of Japanese origin. The very clock upon
> the wall is a deceptive imitation of some masterpiece of
> Japan art, with a gong-like face all embroidered in cloisonné
> enamel, in which the Roman numerals for the hours struggle
> to be understood through the puzzling mimicry of the
> Mongolian alphabet.[2]

In actual fact, the numerals appearing on the dial are not Roman
but Chinese, as are most of the other decorative details. Such
cloisonné clocks were generally made to sit on mantelpiece
shelves, flanked by cloisonné vases that often supported
candelabra. As a hanging wall clock, it has few rivals.

CHRISTOPHER MONKHOUSE

Apollo and Marsyas

1888

Hans Thoma (German, 1839–1924)

Oil on board, in the original frame; 101 x 73.5 cm (30 ¾ x 28 ⅞ in.)

THROUGH PRIOR GIFT OF HENRY MORGAN, ANN G. MORGAN, MEYER WASSER, AND RUTH G. WASSER, 2008.555

HANS THOMA WAS a leading figure in the late-nineteenth-century shift from Realism and history painting to an art inspired by classical myths and legends. Following a childhood in the Black Forest village of Bernau, he pursued artistic study in Karlsruhe and later in Düsseldorf. In 1868 he traveled to Paris, where he became acquainted with Gustave Courbet, whose robust Realist landscapes would provide an important touchstone for his own interpretation of nature. A year later, Thoma met the Swiss artist Arnold Böcklin and, like him, became part of a group known as the Deutschrömer. Active in Italy, this circle of German-speaking painters and sculptors depicted mythical heroes and Teutonic legends as a way to move beyond Realism and French Impressionism, with its emphasis on modern-day subjects.

This intimate yet emotionally charged composition is the last of three in which Thoma represented scenes from Ovid's epic poem *The Metamorphoses*.[1] The work shows the satyr Marsyas challenging the god Apollo, a master of the lyre, to a musical contest. Although the artist did not reveal the cruel outcome of the match—Marsyas lost and was flayed alive—he hinted at the winner through his treatment of Apollo, whose luminous, idealized body sets him apart from his rival, who is cast in shadow. The painted frame, with small vignettes of frogs, grotesque heads, and roosters, may also have been inspired by a tale from *The Metamorphoses*.

In the first two paintings in this series, Thoma used sturdy, heroic figural types that reveal the influence of Böcklin's boldly mythic compositions. In *Apollo and Marsyas*, by contrast, he came closer to the spirit of French Symbolist Pierre Puvis de Chavannes, who was internationally acclaimed for his depictions of languid, elegant figures in arcadian landscapes. In fact, Thoma never completely abandoned his interest in painting directly from nature, and he based the background of this work on a friend's estate outside Rome.[2] *Apollo and Marsyas* was one of three works that the artist exhibited at the Munich Glaspalast in 1889, a year before a show at the city's Kunstverein made his reputation. Early publications of the piece show the painted frame, which like the painting itself was miraculously not damaged during the work's exciting but perilous history. This included sequestration by the Nazis, restitution after the war, and escape from a fire that destroyed a large portion of the collection in which it was held.[3]

GLORIA GROOM

Earthly Paradise

1888

Paul Gauguin (French, 1848–1903)
Emile Bernard (French, 1868–1941)

Painted pine and oak; 101 x 120 x 60.5 cm (39 ¾ x 47 ¼ x 23 ⅞ in.)

Inscribed and dated: *Paul Gauguin* (bottom center); *Emile Bernard* (bottom center); *1888* (bottom left)

THROUGH PRIOR GIFT OF HENRY MORGAN, ANN C. MORGAN, MEYER WASSER, AND RUTH G. WASSER; RESTRICTED GIFT OF EDWARD M. BLAIR, 2007.247

THIS CARVED, PAINTED cabinet, which resulted from the creative collaboration and competition between the Post-Impressionists Paul Gauguin and Emile Bernard, is a unique testament to the era's reevaluation of easel painting. By August 1888, when the forty-one-year-old Gauguin joined the much younger Bernard in Pont-Aven, a village on the coast of Brittany, both artists were already experimenting with nonillusionistic space, flat areas of color, and heavy outlines inspired by earlier decorative traditions such as enamel work, mosaics, and stained glass windows. Not surprisingly, given that they desired to integrate art into everyday life, the pair decided to design a piece of furniture on which they could test out their new ideas. Gauguin, who had been sculpting in wood for over a decade, no doubt instigated the project, lending the younger artist tools and teaching him to carve. Bernard, for his part, was quick to catch on, using the carved line in the same way that he had used outlined and interlocking forms in his paintings. This style is known as *cloisonnism*, and Gauguin was also assimilating it into his own work.[1]

On first viewing, *Earthly Paradise*, a remarkable fusion of painting and sculpture, resembles the heavily carved and polychromed furniture of Brittany. However, its unconventional shape and proportions suggest that it is not a traditional Breton piece but rather an artist-designed work. Gauguin and Bernard carved and painted separate panels that were ultimately pieced together by a furniture maker. Sadly, no correspondence exists to elucidate the details of the cabinet's genesis. The artists must have agreed upon the design, palette, and placement of all the panels, with Gauguin taking on at least three of the five. It is clear that Bernard carved the panel at left because the tightly stacked figures closely resemble the medievalizing woodcuts he began making a few months later.[2] Three of the five panels include motifs—geese, goats, flowering trees, and men and women in traditional costume—that appear in their most important canvases from this same summer: Gauguin's *Vision after the Sermon* (National Gallery of Scotland, Edinburgh) and Bernard's *Bretons in a Prairie* (private collection, France). In the rightmost vertical panel, however, Gauguin signaled his other identity as a painter of the tropics with figures drawn from his trip to Martinique the previous year. It remains uncertain which artist created the bottom panel with the shallow figures of Adam and Eve, which no doubt gave the work its title.

Supplementing the museum's rich collection of Gauguin's paintings and works on paper, *Earthly Paradise* reveals another aspect of his practice and illuminates the role that he and his contemporaries played in reviving the decorative arts. It also reminds viewers of the serial nature of his collaborations: the cabinet would have been completed by October 21, 1888, when Gauguin left Pont Aven for the southern French town of Arles, where he began another competitive, highly productive relationship with Vincent van Gogh.

GLORIA GROOM

Frog-Man (Le Grenouillard)

1892

Jean-Joseph Carriès (French, 1855–1894)

Plaster with reddish brown patina; 34 x 47 x 43 cm
(13 1/2 x 18 1/2 x 17 in.)

THROUGH PRIOR GIFT OF MRS. HENRY WOODS, 2007.78

IN 1892 THE SCULPTOR Jean-Joseph Carriès sent a ceramic version of *Frog-Man* to the Salon National des Beaux-Arts. A powerful example of Symbolist art, it was the most famous of the artist's fabulous froglike creatures, of which the Art Institute's is one of only two known versions in plaster. Carriès was a visionary whose achievement in bronze, ceramics, and plaster is only now being fully explored; in his day, however, he was admired by vanguard artists including Paul Gauguin and recognized by the French nation, which awarded him the rank of chevalier in 1892.

The son of a family of artisans, Carriès studied in Lyon and at the prestigious École des Beaux-Arts in Paris. In 1878, after seeing the Japanese display at the Universal Exposition, he enthusiastically embraced enameled ceramics and stoneware, developing his own nontraditional themes and techniques that combined influences from Japanese and medieval art as well as Symbolist literature. By 1888 he had embarked on a self-imposed exile to Saint-Amande-en-Puisaye, a town known for its potters; there he developed enamel glazes and various methods of rendering a patina, which he considered the "skin of the artwork."[2] Although Carriès displayed the ceramic *Frog-Man* at the 1892 Salon—the first exhibition to allow such minor, "industrial applied arts"—the artist himself made no distinction between his work in different media. Nor could his creations be mass-produced, since he insisted on applying the patina after a piece had been cast or fired,

whether it was a bronze or a plaster like the Art Institute's, which he painted to resemble bronze.

There are important differences between the ceramic *Frog-Man* and the Art Institute's plaster version. The most notable is the presence on the plaster of four frogs, which add a hideous yet comical note to the situation of the half-man, half-batrachian figure whose bug-eyed grimace and pinched lips suggest the force with which he seizes his oversized companion. The work resonates with Darwinian theories of humans emerging from lower life forms, as well as contemporary fears that we might easily slip back into a more primitive state. The frogman's ambiguous expression and the familial clustering of smaller amphibians suggests that he is as much at home in the primeval ooze as out of it. Like Odilon Redon's laughing and crying spiders, whose human qualities make them all the more disturbing, *Frog-Man*, with its beautiful surface that belies a humble medium, presents a similar paradox: a nightmarish, primitive creature that conveys believable human emotions.

GLORIA GROOM

Still Life Filled with Space

1924

Le Corbusier (Charles-Édouard Jeanneret) (French, born
Switzerland, 1887–1965)

Oil on canvas; 60.3 x 73 cm (23 ¾ x 28 ¾ in.)

BEQUEST OF RICHARD S. ZEISLER, 2007.279

IN RESPONSE TO the chaotic social and political climate
following World War I, painter Amédée Ozenfant and
architect Charles-Édouard Jeanneret—better known by
the pseudonym Le Corbusier—called for a change in the
direction of contemporary French art. Criticizing Cubism as
too ornamental, they argued that "the only Art to survive its
era is the art truly rooted in its time" and therefore sought to
promote a new, modern classicism.[1] Calling this style Purism,
Ozenfant, Le Corbusier, and their colleague Fernand Léger
embraced industry and technology, and favored geometrical
forms, logic, mathematical order, and purity over artistic
methodologies that they perceived as "accidental, exceptional,
impressionistic, inorganic, contestatory, [and] picturesque."[2]

Though Le Corbusier is now best known for his
architectural achievements, his effort to develop and promote
Purist aesthetics occupied him intensely between 1918 and
1925.[3] His *Still Life with Space* exemplifies the paintings
he and Ozenfant executed during this period, exploring
the formal visual relationships of mass-produced objects
such as bottles, carafes, coffeepots, glasses, and pipes with
architectural precision.[4] Striving to achieve the geometrical
order that the artists endorsed in their periodical *L'Esprit
nouveau*, Le Corbusier arranged this still life around the axes
of a nearly perfect Cartesian grid, using carefully juxtaposed
planes of color, as opposed to the rules of linear perspective,
to indicate volume and depth.

In order to eliminate the hand of the artist from their
work, the Purists generally painted in a smooth style,
obscuring their brushstrokes. In *Still Life Filled with
Space*, however, Le Corbusier added an unusual amount of
decorative texture, particularly in the patterned border that
he created by dragging a comblike tool repeatedly through
the wet white paint. Moreover, while the human figure had
largely disappeared from Le Corbusier's and Ozenfant's work
by 1921, in this canvas, incidental anthropomorphic forms
emerge from the placement of overlapping and seemingly
transparent objects.[5]

Le Corbusier's deviations from the standard Purist
approach are unexpected, considering that he executed the
picture just one year before he presented the Pavillon de l'Esprit
Nouveau—his "grand summation of Purist aesthetics"—at
the 1925 International Exposition of Modern Decorative
and Industrial Arts in Paris.[6] While these modifications may
embody the integration of humanity and technology that the
Purists envisioned, they also foreshadow Le Corbusier's break
with Ozenfant, the end of Purism as a cohesive intellectual
movement, and the artist's reintroduction of the human figure
in his paintings of the later 1920s.

JILL SHAW

68

Object

1936

Claude Cahun (French, 1894–1954)

Mixed media; 13.7 x 10.7 x 16 cm (5 3/8 x 6 3/8 x 4 in.)

Inscribed: *La Marseillaise est un chant révolutionnaire / La Loi punit le contrefacteur des Travaux forcés* (on base)

THROUGH PRIOR GIFT OF MRS. GILBERT W. CHAPMAN, 2007.30

BORN INTO A literary family, Lucy Schwob began publishing in 1913 under a variety of pseudonyms, consistently adopting the androgynous name Claude Cahun around 1917.[1] With her shaved head and masculine dress, Cahun developed an intriguing artistic persona that challenged traditional notions of gender and sexuality, and her many photographic self-portraits, in which she costumed herself variously as an aviator, a dandy, a sailor, a weightlifter, and a Buddha, likewise blurred conventional constructions of femininity and masculinity.[2] After meeting André Breton in the early 1930s, Cahun became involved with the Surrealists and participated in some of their exhibitions, including the seminal 1936 *Surrealist Exposition of Objects* at the Galerie Charles Ratton in Paris. This enigmatic work—now known as *Object*—was one of three that she produced for the show.[3]

Made of found and constructed items, including pieces of wood, a doll's hand, iron nails, and a tennis ball that was painted and embellished with hair, this small but visually commanding object brings together seemingly diverse elements, much like a collage or Surrealist poem.[4] A cloud intersects an eyeball that is turned on its side and propped up on a stand like a specimen, and a severed doll hand rises from a base bearing the cryptic inscription "The Marseillaise is a revolutionary song. The law punishes the counterfeiter of forced labor."[5] Giving form to many of the preoccupations central to the Surrealists—particularly their fascination with sexuality and the senses of sight and touch—*Object* evokes a number of artistic, cinematic, and literary works created around this time, including Salvador Dalí and Luis Buñuel's Surrealist film *Un Chien andalou* (1929) which famously opens with a woman's eye being slit by a razor and Man Ray's frontispiece for the December 1933 edition of the Surrealist publication *Minotaure*, which incorporates the hands of a mannequin, a billiognave, and one of the artist's photographs featuring a woman's mascara-caked eyes crying glass tears.[6]

Beyond evoking Surrealist visual and literary iconographies, Cahun's assemblage also disrupts traditional definitions of fine art and its production. "I insist on a primary truth," she wrote in 1936. "One has to discover, handle, *tame*, fabricate irrational objects oneself in order to appreciate the particular or general value of those we see before us. That's why, in certain respects, *manual* workers would be better placed than intellectuals to make sense of them."[7] Blurring the lines between high and low culture and promoting an accessible mode of artistic expression that could be practiced by professional and amateur artists alike, Cahun—in rare objects such as this one—destabilized conventional understandings of beauty and identity, artistic media and subject matter.[8]

JILL SHAW

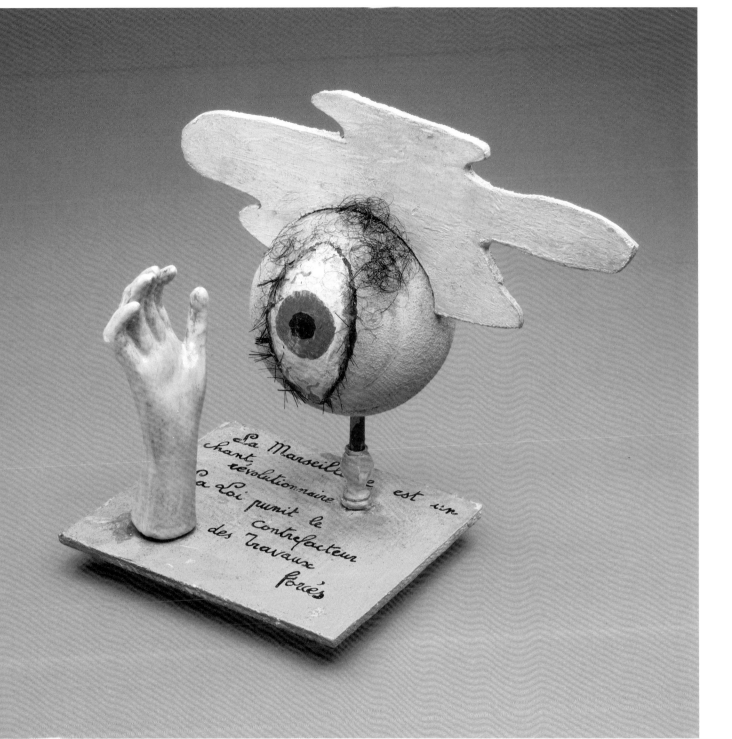

La Marseillaise est un chant révolutionnaire La Loi punit le Contrefacteur des Travaux forcés

Self-Portrait with Camera

c. 1917

Edward Steichen (American, born Luxembourg, 1879–1973)

Platinum print; image: 25 x 19.8 cm (9 ¹³/₁₆ x 7 ¹³/₁₆ in.)

RESTRICTED GIFTS OF BRENDA AND EARL SHAPIRO AND THE SMART FAMILY FOUNDATION; LAURA T. MAGNUSON ACQUISITION, COMER FOUNDATION, THE MARY AND LEIGH BLOCK ENDOWMENT FUNDS; RESTRICTED GIFTS OF SIDNEY AND SONDRA BERMAN EPSTEIN, KAREN AND JIM FRANK, MARIAN PAWLICK; ETHEL T. SCARBOROUGH, HUGH LEANDER AND MARY TRUMBULL ADAMS MEMORIAL ENDOWMENT, BETTY BELL SPOONER FUNDS; RESTRICTED GIFTS OF VICKI AND THOMAS HORWICH, ROBIN AND SANDY STUART; SAMUEL A. MARX PURCHASE FUND FOR MAJOR ACQUISITIONS, S. DEWITT CLOUGH, PHOTOGRAPHIC SOCIETY, IRVING AND JUNE SEAMAN ENDOWMENT, MORRIS L. PARKER FUNDS. 2008.243

INITIALLY TRAINED AS a painter, in 1902 Edward Steichen became actively involved with the Photo-Secession, a group of amateur practitioners led by Alfred Stieglitz that aspired to have photography recognized as an art. With a penchant for the hand-crafted print, the Photo-Secessionists often employed a sentimental, soft-focus aesthetic that blurred distinctions between their photographs and works in other media such as painting, printmaking, and drawing. Indeed, in a 1902 self-portrait (right), Steichen presented himself as a painter, and a review that year noted: "The position of [his] hand, with long fingers, grasping a brush, shows great flexibility of purpose and work, a power which is accentuated by the subtle curve as though the brush had been used."[1] Indeed, the artist's chosen printing process—gum dichromate, in which the emulsion could be manipulated with a brush—was itself painterly, displaying a degree of tactility and handiwork more commonly associated with lithography or other nonphotographic processes.

It is all the more striking, then, to see this later self-portrait (far right), in which Steichen seems to resolutely declare himself a photographer. Posing confidently with his large-format camera, he utilized a crisp aesthetic and straightforward printing process in this self-assessment, which he made at a pivotal moment in his career. By 1917 Steichen had stopped painting, had distanced himself from the Photo-Secession, and—although he had played an active role in Stieglitz's gallery, 291—had broken decisively with his mentor in reaction to a disagreement about World War I. Nevertheless, Steichen's more clean and modern sensibility coincided with a similar directness of approach adopted by Stieglitz, Paul Strand, and other key American photographers.

Steichen's receptivity to his medium's different styles and possible functions was a hallmark of a career that also encompassed making photographs for the United States military and fashion spreads for Condé Nast magazines, and curating popular photography exhibitions at the Museum of Modern Art, New York. He signaled this openness in his response to a 1915 questionnaire from Stieglitz, declaring his wish that photography galleries should "never have anything resembling a constitution or an eternal policy, for the very good reason that any one of these would be sufficient to dull its receptivity to new elements . . . there is no permanent room for dogma or even the trace of anything that moves toward dogma."[2]

KATHERINE BUSSARD

Edward Steichen. *Self-Portrait with Brush and Palette*, 1902. Gum dichromate print; 26.7 x 20 cm (10 ½ x 7 ⅞ in.). Alfred Stieglitz Collection, 1949.823.

Satiric Dancer

1926

André Kertész (American, born Hungary, 1894–1985)

Gelatin silver print; 9 x 7.8 cm (3 $^9/_{16}$ x 3 $^1/_{16}$ in.)

GIFT OF NICHOLAS AND SUSAN PRITZKER, OBJ. 199268

ANDRÉ KERTÉSZ, WIDELY considered one of the greatest photographers of all time, first gained attention in Paris during the later 1920s, as a leader among a new generation of artist-photographers who thrived in print and at exhibition. Kertész created work suitable for an international array of widely read illustrated magazines that also earned the esteem of the Parisian artistic elite. His photographs responded to popular cultural expectations as well as new ideas in high culture, and in their exquisite subtlety held an appeal that remains keenly appreciated today.

Two views of the dancer Magda Förstner posing in the Montparnasse studio of sculptor Étienne Beöthy exemplify Kertész's approach. In the Art Institute's photograph (left), Förstner—clad in a short halter dress with a ruff around her neck—perches alluringly on a couch, her lower legs swiveled outward as if in imitation of a Charleston step.[1] Her angled limbs and splayed fingers suggest a centripetal force that counteracts the perspective collapse generated by the receding lines of the floorboards and walls. Förstner and Beöthy belonged to the creative circle of fellow Hungarian emigrés that provided Kertész with his closest companionship and greatest artistic influence during his early years in Paris. Beöthy was pursuing an abstracted figural language in sculpture, just as Kertész was in photography, and his statue, *Direct Action*, which appears in a corner next to the sofa, serves as a foil for the latter's camera work.

French poet Paul Dermée wrote of Kertész that his "retinas become virgin again at each blink."[2] In fact, here and in many other Parisian works Kertész explores the tensions between immaculate vision and knowing insight. The photographs that he took in Beöthy's studio present a magnetic conflict between chastity and carnality as embodied in two creatures of similar appearance: the Apollonian, sexless nude in bleached white stone and the seductively clothed, Dionysian "satyr" with alabaster skin.

The other image taken at this session (right) appeared in the Berlin leisure magazine *Die Dame* in 1927, illustrating a fictional dialogue on marital infidelity entitled "Kleine Lügen" (Small Lies).[3] Several months later, Kertész held his first art gallery exhibition, for which Dermée wrote the words quoted earlier. Although neither of the *Satiric Dancer* photographs appeared in this show, they were in keeping with Kertész's still

lifes, artists' portraits, and studio views (for example, of Piet Mondrian's atelier) that were paired with geometric abstractions by a Hungarian painter named Ida Thal. It is easy to imagine that the compression of a sculpture, a living person, and a living room into a flattened wedge of pictorial space might capture the imagination of the artists with whom Kertész associated, just as it is easy to see how the charm of Förstner's pose excited a much broader public imagination in print.

The version published in 1927 became an icon of art photography, and possibly gained its current title, only toward the end of Kertész's life, when he recovered the negative and reprinted it many times, repeatedly ranking it among his most prized works.[4] The artist is believed to have made only one print during his lifetime, meanwhile, of the version at the Art Institute. Compositionally, it is equally stunning, and, with its reference to the Charleston, may be more pointed in its dialogue with popular culture. Contemplating this play of lines of force, peering at the protagonists in this miniaturized drama of fleshly fantasy and purist abstraction, one feels not so much restored to innocence as pushed and pulled into a throbbing consciousness of life.

MATTHEW S. WITKOVSKY

Andre Kertesz. *Satiric Dancer*, 1926. Gelatin silver print; 10.5 x 7.9 cm (4 ⅛ x 3 ⅛ in.). Collection of Nicholas and Susan Pritzker.

Study for "Let's Return the Country's Coal Debt"

1930

Gustav Klutsis (Russian, 1895—1938)

Gelatin silver print with gouache; 15.9 x 11.1 cm (6 ¼ x 4 ⅜ in.)

GLADYS N. ANDERSON FUND. 133.2009

Worker Men and Women: Everyone Vote in the Soviet Elections

1930

Gustav Klutsis

Lithograph; 119.4 x 83.8 cm (47 x 33 in.)

Published in Moscow by Izogiz, edition of 10,000

ADA TURNBULL HERTLE FUND. 132.2009

GUSTAV KLUTSIS WAS one of the foremost practitioners of propaganda art, which uses images and words as instruments of political persuasion. Born Gustavs Klucis in Latvia, he trained in painting at the Academy of Fine Arts in Riga—at that time part of the Russian Empire. Drafted into the Imperial Army, the artist took part in the military revolt that toppled Czar Nicholas II and came to Moscow in 1918 as part of a detachment of soldiers assigned to guard the Kremlin, the new seat of power in Russia.

Klutsis resumed making art in 1919, this time at the center of the avant-garde. For most of the 1920s, he studied or taught at Vkhutemas (Higher State Artistic and Technical Workshops), a government-funded school of art, architecture, and design that was part of Lenin's plan to involve artists in engineering the post-revolutionary Russian state, both practically and symbolically. A set of theoretical and artistic propositions grouped under the term *Constructivism* came to dominate teaching at Vkhutemas, spreading outward to have an enormous international impact in the 1920s and later.[1]

Like others in the Constructivist orbit, notably El Lissitzky, Aleksandr Rodchenko, and Varvara Stepanova, Klutsis soon turned to photomontage, and made cut-and-pasted photographs his primary technique from the mid-1920s. He achieved his greatest results between 1928 and 1932, designing a series of exhibition displays, murals, posters, and publications in a uniquely impressive idiom that, as Joseph Goebbels, the Nazi propaganda minister, supposedly commented, would convince anyone of the victory of communism.[2] Klutsis took his own photographs, often posing himself and his friends in the desired roles, in what may be interpreted as an attempt to insert himself into the image of history in the making. The censors at the state publishing house, Izogiz, frequently responded by making him redo his designs. Klutsis also tested multiple exposures and "sandwiched" negatives to create an effect of bodies layered into an indivisible whole, as in the hand-painted photographic study for the poster *Let's Return the Country's Coal Debt (Vernem ugol'nyi dolg strane)* with its trio of workers striding in lockstep. In other instances, such as the Art Institute's lithograph, he repeated single images—for example, the pyramid of seemingly innumerable hands, all his own, that surge and pulse toward the slogan "Worker Men

and Women: Everyone Vote in the Soviet Elections" (Raboche I rabotnisty: vse na perevybory sovetov)—to guarantee the uniformity of the proletariat, voicing their ideas as one.

These two pieces are part of a recently acquired group of twenty-five works by Klutsis, including the published version of *Let's Return the Country's Coal Debt*. These belong, in turn, to a much larger acquisition of several hundred items from the collection of Robert and June Leibowits, made possible by a major collaborative initiative of the departments of Photography, Prints and Drawings, and Architecture and Design, and the Ryerson Library. The Leibowits holdings tell a remarkable story of avant-garde art across media in early-twentieth-century central and eastern Europe. They are concentrated on Russian Futurism and on the avant-garde milieux of Czechoslovakia, Germany, the Netherlands, and Soviet Russia in the 1920s and 1930s, and include a premier group of Russian Futurist books; objects and maquettes for advertising and design from the Bauhaus, De Stijl, and international exponents of Constructivism; a large number of pieces from the Czech avant-garde; and strong bodies of work from key innovators including photomontage agitator John Heartfield, artist and architect El Lissitzky, and designers Ladislav Sutnar, Karel Teige, and Piet Zwart.

MATTHEW S. WITKOVSKY

77

Near Jackson, Mississippi

C. 1970

William Eggleston (American, born 1939)

Dye imbibition print; 55.3 x 36 cm (21 3/4 x 14 3/16 in.)

RESTRICTED GIFT OF ROBERT AND JOAN FEITLER, 2006.326

WHETHER A PENSIVE consideration of a simple house-hold object like an oven or an exercise in the abstracted American palette of red, white, and blue as found in a child-ren's jacket, a color photograph by William Eggleston represents a revolution in contemporary practice. Well into the 1970s, exhibitions of black-and-white photographs dominated the discourse of art photography, and color images, as art critic Janet Malcolm wrote at the time, were associated with the medium's "most retrograde applications—advertising, fashion, [and] *National Geographic*-type travel pictures."[1] Attempting to explain Eggleston's color photographs in relation to art, Malcolm characterized them as deficient reprisals of Photorealist paintings.

Curator John Szarkowski, by contrast, recognized Eggleston's contribution and organized *William Eggleston's Guide*, which opened at the Museum of Modern Art, New York, in 1976. Eggleston took the pictures in this exhibition and its catalogue almost exclusively in his native South. Of these photographs, Szarkowski wrote: "[They] seem to me perfect: irreducible surrogates for the experience they pretend to record, visual analogues for the quality of one life, collectively a paradigm of a private view, a view one would have thought ineffable, described here with clarity, fullness, and elegance."[2]

In 1959 an encounter with the work of Henri Cartier-Bresson spurred Eggleston to practice photography more rigorously. He blended the compositional formality of Cartier-Bresson's aesthetic with a remarkable openness to his southern subject matter. The idea of focusing his camera on his native surroundings was fueled by his dislike for his local culture.[3] In 1965 Eggleston began taking photographs on negative color film and was soon working exclusively in color, producing rich, saturated dye-transfer prints. For a generation of photographers that included William Christenberry, Joel Meyerowitz, John Pfahl, and Stephen Shore, his 1976 exhibition affirmed that serious artistic work could be made in color, and that such work could draw on commonplace experiences of unassuming subjects. Eggleston's photographs are thus the necessary preamble to the later work of such talents as Nan Goldin, Richard Misrach, and Alec Soth.

Creating photographs studiously extracted from the everyday, color-filled world, Eggleston established himself as the foundational figure in the art of color photography. *Near Jackson, Mississippi*—the closing plate of his carefully sequenced *Guide* catalogue—joins five other of his photographs already in the Art Institute's collection.[4]

KATHERINE BUSSARD

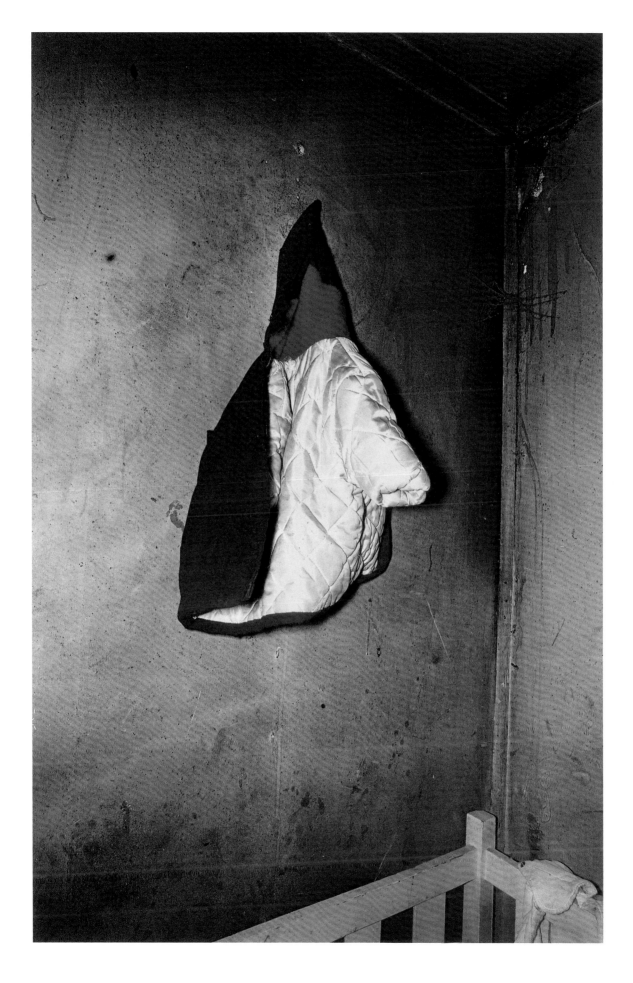

The Nativity and Coffer

c. 1490

Master of the Very Small Hours of Anne of Brittany (Master of the Unicorn Hunt) (French, active 1480–1510)

Woodcut: hand colored with brush, stencil, and watercolor on ivory laid paper; image: 16.4 x 23.1 cm (6 7/16 x 9 1/8 in.)

Coffer: wood, iron, leather, linen, and horsehair; 22 x 33 x 15 cm (8 5/8 x 13 x 5 15/16 in.)

Inscribed: *Mirabile mysterium declaratur hodie, innovantur naturae; Deus homo factus est; id quod fuit, permansit, et quod non erat, assumpsit, non commixtionem passus [neque divisionem].* (A wondrous mystery is declared today, an innovation is made upon nature; God is made man; that which he was, he remains, and that which he was not, he takes on, suffering neither commixture nor division; in the block below the image)

GEORGE F. HARDING DEACCESSIONS FUND; RESTRICTED GIFT OF MR. AND MRS. WILLIAM VANCE; THE AMANDA S. JOHNSON AND MARION J. LIVINGSTON FUND, 2009.49

LATE FIFTEENTH-CENTURY French safety boxes, or coffers, are hybrid artifacts that can provide unique insight into the use and function of prints during the first century of their invention. Constructed in a variety of sizes, these handsome wooden containers are covered in leather and reinforced with iron straps; decorative metalwork surrounds the clasps and locks on the most elaborate examples. The inside covers are often adorned with hand-colored woodcuts of religious subjects. Because only one hundred or so print-adorned coffers of this period survive, the appearance at auction of a private collection of twenty-two boxes offered the Art Institute of Chicago an extraordinary—and possibly final—chance to select an example for the collection.[1] Pictured here is the unusually large and complete coffer acquired jointly by the Department of Medieval through Modern Painting and Sculpture and the Department of Prints and Drawings.[2]

The woodcut images in the coffers are Parisian, and most are known only in association with these boxes. Among them, the most refined are attributed to the Master of the Very Small Hours of Anne of Brittany, named for one of his masterworks, an illuminated book in the Bibliothèque Nationale de France, Paris. A designer of manuscript illuminations, woodcuts, stained glass, and tapestries, this artist was also closely involved with Parisian printers of books of hours.[3] He is also called the Master of the Unicorn Hunt after his famous *Unicorn Tapestries* (c. 1495–1505; Musée National du Moyen Age, Paris, and Metropolitan Museum of Art, New York) and Master of the Apocalypse Rose for his design of the great rose window for Sainte-Chapelle, Paris.[4] The fresh and bright Nativity woodcut that adorns the Art Institute's box is part of a series depicting the life of Christ; it must have been one of this master's most popular compositions, because at least twelve impressions survive.[5]

Coffers of this type served their original function for a short span of time, between about 1480 and 1510. They were created almost exclusively in Paris, perhaps by vendors working near the Sorbonne, where the book, stationery, and print trades were based.[6] A new study incorporating technical analysis of the materials, construction, and wear patterns of the boxes suggests that although once called messenger boxes, these coffers were not built to withstand long-distance travel but rather were designed for local transport, perhaps from one parish church to another. The nature of their contents remains somewhat unclear, but they seem likely to have had a liturgical function. The woodcuts would have facilitated this usage: when the lid was raised, the casket could serve as a small altar for personal devotion. The leather and horsehair cushion on the bottom of this example would have made the bearer more comfortable when carrying the coffer on his back with leather straps. Like some of the other boxes, the Art Institute's container has a shallow hidden compartment in its lid, accessible by removing a tiny nail, that appears to have been impossible to open and close easily; therefore, it must have been designed, as reliquaries were, to safeguard something of value that did not need to be removed on a regular basis to serve its purpose. Once they ceased to fulfill their original function, the boxes were used to store books, papers, trinkets, and family heirlooms.[8] Although this coffer and its surviving counterparts remain mysterious, their study promises compelling new information about the social history and material culture of early modern France.

MARTHA TEDESCHI

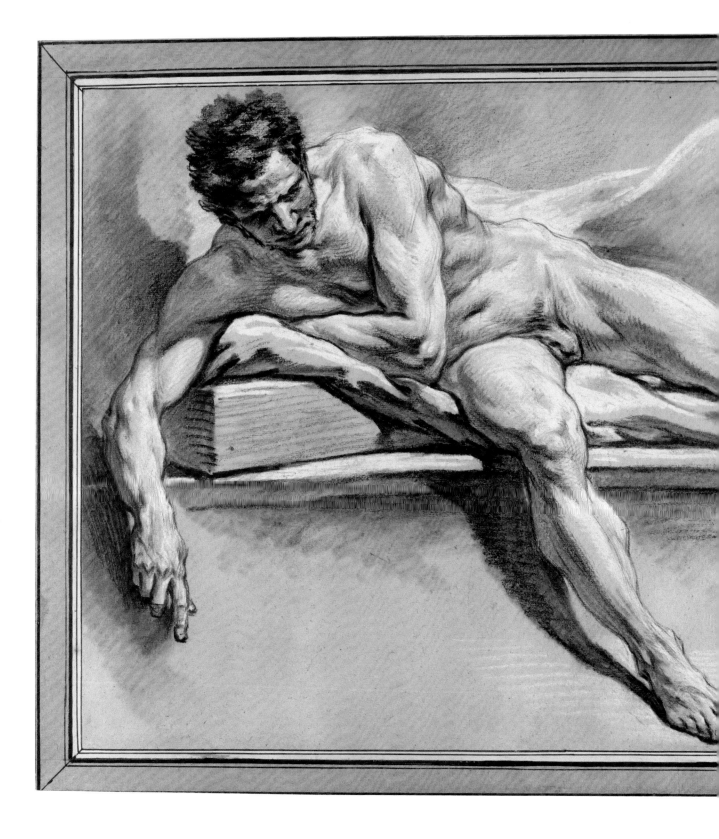

Academic Study of a Reclining Male Nude

C. 1750

François Boucher (French, 1703–1770)

Black chalk with stumping, heightened with white chalk, red chalk, and black pastel (?) on buff laid paper, on an eighteenth-century mount; 35.6 x 44.8 cm (14 x 17 ⅝ in.)

REGENSTEIN ENDOWMENT, 2009.42

DRAWING EFFECTIVELY FROM a live, nude male model was one of the basic requirements of all academic training. Students usually executed figure drawings in red chalk, often working from the same model.[1] Paradoxically, it was believed that the more closely a young artist conformed to this regulated ideal, the more likely he was to succeed as an original painter.[2]

François Boucher was one of the most talented, prolific, and versatile French artists of the eighteenth century. His influence was immense in part because he occupied a series of increasingly important positions at the Royal Academy of Painting and Sculpture. There he oversaw life-drawing sessions and the production of *académies*. These drawn studies from life were themselves copied by students, as well as transformed into etchings for distribution to provincial centers as models for instruction. Around 1750, Louis Félix de La Rue produced a set of such etchings showing male nudes in contemplative poses.

Having appeared on the market only recently, this spectacular work, executed in three chalks, has been heralded as "a dazzling demonstration of [Boucher's] technique."[3] Two other significant versions of this composition exist.[4] A red chalk académie in the Musée du Louvre, Paris, shows the figure in almost the same position.[5] Another three-chalk version, now in a private Canadian collection, includes a more complicated description of the drapery behind the figure and artist's materials on the ground.[6]

Close comparison of these studies suggests that the Louvre académie was created first, followed by the Art Institute's sheet, and then the Canadian drawing.[7] The Chicago académie was clearly the basis for La Rue's etching: the treatment of the drapery is the same as that in the print, and telling pentimenti in the index finger and around the right ankle reinforce this conviction. Boucher must have felt it necessary to ennoble the setting for the etched series, for he introduced a huge tome. The Canadian sheet must have followed, as it is drawn without pentimenti, and the setting is further elaborated.[8]

Although the Art Institute's version served as a model for La Rue's etched series, it was probably not actively used for teaching purposes. Rather, like the Canadian académie, it was intended to appeal to a nascent group of collectors who framed and hung such studies as works of art. Indeed, at least one of them caught the attention of Boucher's most ardent collector, Jean-Claude Gaspard de Sireul, who is said to have owned over two hundred drawings and sixteen paintings by the artist. While it is impossible to know which of the three-chalk drawings—the one in Chicago or the one in Canada—was in Sireul's possession, both reveal the elevation of the académie from mere studio practice to a framed, virtuoso presentation of the idealized male form.[9]

SUZANNE FOLDS McCULLAGH

Bathers

1928

Max Beckmann (German, 1884–1950)

Inscribed: *Beckmann / Scheuveningen / 28* (lower right, in black pastel)

Black, white, and yellow pastel, with touches of black Conté crayon and stumping on tan wove paper prepared with blue gouache; 88.1 x 58.7 cm (34 11/16 x 23 1/8 in.)

GIFT OF MR. AND MRS. STANLEY M. FREEHLING, 1964.202

DIFFICULT TO SUCCINCTLY characterize, Max Beckmann's work spanned a wide variety of styles and artistic movements ranging from Impressionism to New Objectivity. The artist launched his career after the turn of the twentieth century, working in a modified Impressionist vein and garnering attention and renown through his frequent exhibitions at the Berlin Secession and the gallery of Paul Cassirer, an esteemed dealer in that city. But Beckmann's experience as a medical orderly in World War I precipitated a dramatic shift in his work. After he suffered a nervous breakdown in 1915, the artist began to display a raw, claustrophobic sensibility in his paintings, prints, and drawings, utilizing dramatic disruptions of space and focusing on socially relevant and psychically disturbing themes.

By the mid-1920s, Germany's political situation stabilized, as did Beckmann's own life. He was appointed professor at the Städel Institute in Frankfurt am Main and left a tumultuous relationship with his first wife to marry the younger Mathilde von Kaulbach. Yet even with this steadying of his circumstances, Beckmann continued to embrace pictorial instability in his works and imbue them with a strong sense of social urgency.[1]

One year later, he created the monumental drawing *Bathers*. The scene represents a frolicking group of men and women at Scheuveningen, a popular Dutch resort where he vacationed with his family in October 1928. While the majority of the artist's bather pictures from this period are infused with a characteristic sense of allegory and disturbing sexuality, this composition is surprisingly joyous and lighthearted, as if it depicts a fond memory.[2] Since the beginning of the century, bathing culture took on greater cultural importance in Northern Europe, providing a means for urbanites to reconnect with nature and enjoy the benefits of physical fitness.

Beckmann prepared the ground of this powerful sheet with a vibrant blue gouache that he then worked over with black, white, and yellow pastel and black Conté crayon. Although the large scale of this drawing is not unprecedented in his oeuvre, the deep, rich hue is unusual. As is often the case with his works of this period, the figures are stacked in a vertical format with minimal spatial recession. The two women in the foreground—one resembling Beckmann's wife—hold hands as if dancing in the waves, while further back, male bathers join the fun. The stripes on their bathing costumes resemble those captured in a 1928 photograph of Beckmann on the Scheuveningen beach.[3] It is therefore possible that the drawing is a modified family portrait, documenting the Beckmanns' fall seaside vacation.

JAY A. CLARKE

Untitled 6/20/89

1989

Carroll Dunham (American, born 1949)

Green, yellow, and red wax crayon, with graphite, on ivory wove paper, 45.7 x 60 cm (18 x 23 ⅝ in.)

MARGARET FISHER ENDOWMENT FUND, 2007.500

NEW YORK-BASED ARTIST Carroll Dunham has distinguished himself as one of the outstanding draftsmen of his generation. Over the course of his career, he has employed a lexicon of marks and shapes that range in character from pseudopornographic crudeness to extreme refinement, from random doodling to precise rendering—usually within the same work. His drawings make constant references to natural forms, such as bodily orifices, mutating cells, and sexual and internal organs.[1]

At the Art Institute's invitation, the artist assembled twenty works completed between 1989 and 2006 that summarize his breadth as a draftsman and document his graphic evolution. Of these, *Untitled 6/20/89* is a particularly strong example and comes first chronologically.[2] All of the shapes in this drawing are vaguely familiar: conglomerations of organic and cellular forms (some suggesting human anatomy) that commingle, conjoin, float, and attach themselves to the edges of the composition. The artist has said that all of his visual ideas progress from a daily drawing practice that is at once rigorously formal and ridiculously playful, generating automatic markings or doodles that reveal directions, rhythms, or motifs he can develop further. In *Untitled 6/20/89*, Dunham explored several elements that recur in his work of this period, including the central form, created by a single meandering line and embellished with marks akin to antennae, hair follicles, or perhaps acne. Quick graphite scribbles resembling clouds, burning flowers, and swimming sperm complete the composition.

As is generally the case with Dunham's drawings, these fields of clashing shapes elude specific narrative readings, but they have been interpreted formally as statements about the properties of picture making, and psychologically as manifestations of the artist's subconscious. These interpretations deserve special credence considering Dunham's self-consciously automatist approach and his confessed indebtedness to the Surrealists; he has admitted that as a teenager he was attracted to the work of Yves Tanguy and Salvador Dalí, and later to Matta's.[3] However, it would be inaccurate to align Dunham only with Surrealism. Like most contemporary artists, his influences are numerous and diverse. Indeed, his graphic vocabulary is informed by canonical twentieth-century artists like Vasily Kandinsky and Joan Miró; peers such as Philip Guston and Cy Twombly; popular comics and animated cartoons; and children's drawings, with their uninhibited nature.[4]

EMILY VOKT ZIEMBA AND MARK PASCALE

'89 Udine

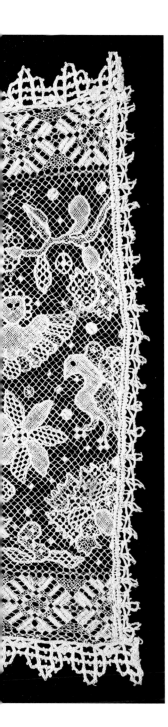

Panel

17th century

Germany, Hamburg

Linen, knotted netting embroidered with cloth, interlocking lace, buttonhole stitches, and woven wheels (lacis construction); edged on all sides with attached bobbin lace; 40 x 57 cm (15 ¾ x 22 ⁷/₁₆ in.)

RESTRICTED GIFT OF THE ANTIQUARIAN SOCIETY, SHIRLEY WELSH RYAN, MARLENE K. PHILLIPS, ROSEMARIE BUNTROCK, BARBARA FRANKE, THE TEXTILE SOCIETY OF THE ART INSTITUTE OF CHICAGO, AND FRIENDS IN MEMORY AND HONOR OF ALICE WELSH SKILLING, FORMER PRESIDENT OF THE TEXTILE SOCIETY, 2001–2005, 2008.168

IN THIS PANEL, possibly used as a bridal pillow or to commemorate a marriage, a symmetrical composition of birds, cherubs, deer, and sprigs of flowers surrounds a male figure encircled by a length of cloth and surmounted by a crown.[1] A repeating motif of blooms, possibly carnations, forms the upper and lower borders, and bobbin lace trim runs along the edges of the piece. This delicate object was created with needlework stitches and lace techniques on a ground of lacis construction, a method of hand knotting that is used to create a square- or lozenge-grid pattern of netting. Considered one of the oldest lace-making techniques, this structure evolved from knotting methods traditionally used in fishing nets and animal snares. It was later appropriated as a ground for ornamental embellishment throughout Europe, reaching its greatest popularity in the sixteenth and seventeenth centuries.[2]

This work belongs to a group of related German lacis pieces with similar dimensions and motifs that were produced with only minor variation over the course of three hundred years, from the seventeenth to the nineteenth century.[3] Several of these are nearly identical, displaying couples or kissing birds. Although the powerful male figure of this particular panel does not correspond with typical matrimonial imagery, he may depict an unidentified mythological figure.

The source of such designs is elusive, but they may have come from the multitude of pattern books for lace and needlework that were published widely from the early sixteenth to the early eighteenth century, especially in Frankfurt and Nuremberg.[4] Many included— or were entirely composed of—grid patterns, which were in some cases specifically designed for lacis work. For example, the *Model-buchs* of 1676, published in Nuremberg, illustrates numerous patterns that could have easily been adapted and combined to form the sprigs of flowers found in this panel. The same volume includes a fold-out pattern in the same style, size, and layout as the German lacis works mentioned above, including the Art Institute's example. Indeed, the stylistic consistency of these pieces may be due to the fact that they were based on, or directly copied from, any number of pattern books that were reused over the centuries.

ODILE V. JOASSIN

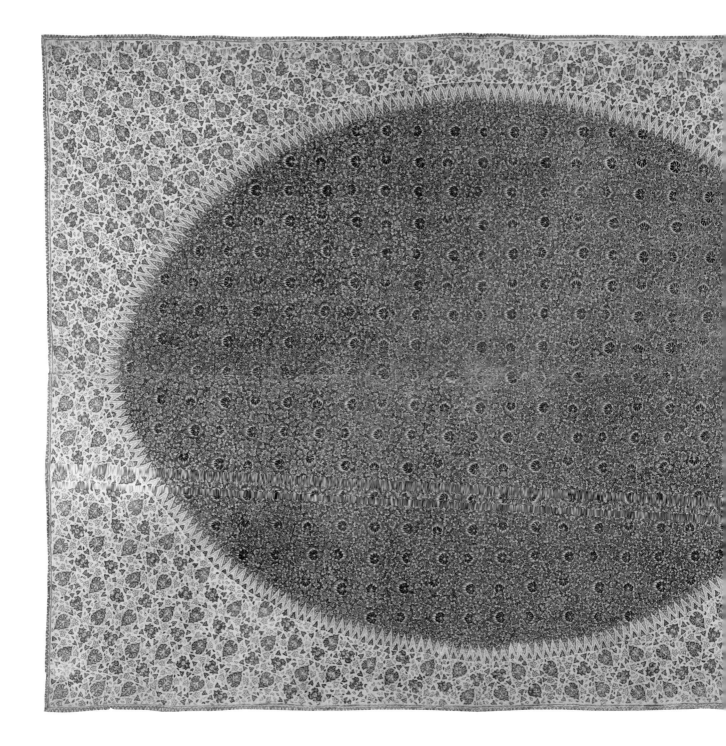

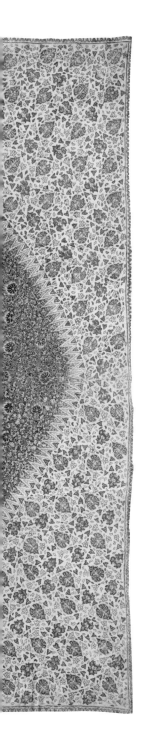

Ceremonial Skirt Cloth (Dodot)

17th century

India, Coromandel Coast, for the Sumatran market

Two panels joined: cotton, plain weave; hand-drawn mordant and resist-dyed; 346.4 x 239.1 cm (136 3/8 x 94 1/8 in.)

RESTRICTED GIFT OF THE ALSDORF FOUNDATION; JAMES AND MARILYNN ALSDORF ACQUISITION FUND, 2008.669

INDIA AND THE Indonesian Archipelago have a centuries-old tradition of exchanging goods and ideas through maritime trade. Indian merchants shipped many commodities to Indonesia in return for items such as spices. Of these exports, textiles stood out as highly esteemed symbols of social prestige. Using various techniques, weavers created distinct designs for specific Indonesian clienteles. This ceremonial skirt cloth, or *dodot*, was among those made for the Javanese and Sumatran markets. A Javanese textile form, this example was imported to Sumatra during the dominance of the Javanese Mataram Empire, which influenced the island's religion, social structure, and courtly ritual to a great degree.[1]

The Art Institute's dodot exemplifies the complexity of mordant-painted textiles imported from India's Coromandel Coast, a major textile producing region, during its peak in the seventeenth century. A mordant, in this case a metallic oxide, is an agent used to bond a dye to the surface of a textile. The complex technique of direct mordanting was exclusive to the Indian Subcontinent, making such pieces highly desirable. This monopoly ended when the Dutch brought mordanting to Europe in the late 1600s.[2]

Composed of two lengths of woven cotton sewn together, this dodot's delicate floral motifs are set in an oval on a rectangular cloth. The dense patterning of the oval consists of lotus blossoms surrounded by arabesque designs on a red background. The lotus motif continues in the area outside the oval, which features small flowers and petals over a swirling background of fine lines. Although the lotus has long been associated with Indian art traditions, most recognizably Hindu-Buddhist iconography, the center and the eight petals that surround it also represent the central axis and eight compass points found in Southeast Asian art.[3] The motif appears frequently in Javanese art, where the orientation or design of the flowers forms directional patterns that represent creation and re-creation.[4]

Although this piece has the form of a Javanese dodot wrap, it was likely used as a canopy or backdrop for ceremonial occasions, as such textiles were not necessarily worn at court but rather used as prestigious decorations. Indeed, many Indian-made dodots show extensive wear in their corners as a result of hanging.[5] However these richly detailed products were used, they were treasured as venerated heirlooms that marked the wealth and importance of their owners.[6]

ODILE V. JOASSIN

NOTES

Vessel with Bird and Peccary Heads, pp. 6–7

1. For information on late Classic Maya ceramics used for royal feasting and gift-giving, see Dorie Reents-Budet, "Feasting among the Classic Maya: Evidence from the Pictorial Ceramics" in *The Maya Vase Book*, ed. Barbara and Justin Kerr (Kerr Associates, 2000), vol. 6, pp. 1022–37; and Dorie Reents-Budet, "Functions of Classic Period Painted Pottery," in *Painting the Maya Universe: Royal Ceramics of the Classic Period* (Duke University Press, 1994), pp. 72–105.
2. For information on Pre-Classic and Early Classic Maya art and culture, see Virginia M. Fields and Dorie Reents-Budet, eds., *Lords of Creation: The Origins of Sacred Maya Kingship* (Los Angeles County Museum of Art/Scala, 2005).
3. For further information on ancient Maya representations of cormorants and their symbolism, see Reents-Budet, *Painting the Maya Universe* (note 1), pp. 244–48; and Fields and Reents-Budet (note 2), cats. 31, 32, 53, 103.
4. For a reconstruction of the ancient Maya creation mythology, see David Freidel, Linda Schele, and Joy Parker, *Maya Cosmos: Three Thousand Years on the Shaman's Path* (Harper Collins, 1993).
5. Linda Schele and Mary Ellen Miller, *The Blood of Kings: Dynasty and Ritual in Maya Art* (Kimbell Art Museum, 1986), p. 280.
6. Floyd Lounsbury, personal communication, cited in Mary Ellen Miller, *The Murals of Bonampak* (Princeton University Press, 1986), pp. 46–50, and Freidel, Schele, and Parker (note 4), pp. 79–84.
7. This constellation is adjacent to one of the places where the ecliptic crosses the Milky Way. On the opposite side of the Milky Way is the Belt of Orion—seen by some Maya as a turtle bearing three hearthstones. During creation, the maize god emerged from a crack in the back of this turtle, just as a stalk of maize rises from the earth. Freidel, Schele, and Parker (note 4), pp. 82–85.

Headdress for Gelede (Igi), pp. 8–9

1. Henry John Drewal, "Gelede Masquerade: Imagery and Motif," *African Arts* 7, 4 (Summer 1974), p. 8.
2. The almost identical mate to this headdress is in the collection of the Yale University Art Gallery (2004.60.1). See "Acquisitions," *Yale University Art Gallery Bulletin* 2005, pp. 137, 139.

Snake Headdress (a-Mantsho-ña-Tshol or Inap), pp. 10–11

1. Frederick Lamp, *Art of the Baga: A Drama of Cultural Reinvention*, exh. cat. (Museum of African Art/Prestel Verlag, 1996), pp. 77, 83.
2. Ibid., p. 84.
3. Ibid., p. 77.
4. For more on these events as they relate to the arts, see ibid., "The Islamic Watershed: A Culture Held in Reserve 1955–1985," pp. 223–39.

5. For a brief biography of Newman, see Alan G. Artner, "Muriel Kallis Steinberg Newman, Modern Art Collector Dies at Age 94," *Chicago Tribune*, Aug. 26, 2008.
6. Like Newman, Pierre Matisse—collector, gallery owner, and son of artist Henri Matisse—purchased a Baga serpent headdress in the 1960s. See Sotheby's, New York, *African, Oceanic and Pre-Columbian Art including Property from the Bareiss, Bohlen and Dinhofer Collections*, sale cat. (Sothebys, May 16, 2008), lot 58, pp. 96–105.
7. Michael FitzGerald, "A Contemporary Sensibility: Pierre Matisse's Intermingling of Tribal Objects and the Western Avant-Garde," in ibid., p. 95.

Polychrome Jar, pp. 12–13

1. The Southwestern ceramic tradition has long been a subject of intense interest. Publications on this topic include Jesse Walter Fewkes, "The Pottery of Sityatki," in *Archaeological Expedition to Arizona in 1895*, Seventeenth Annual Report of the Bureau of American Ethnology (Smithsonian Institution, 1895); Ruth Bunzel, *The Pueblo Potter: A Study of Creative Imagination in Primitive Art* (Columbia University Press, 1929); Alfred Dittert, Jr., and Fred Plog, *Generations in Clay: Pueblo Pottery of the American Southwest* (Northland Press, 1980); David L. Arnold, "Pueblo Pottery: 2,000 Years of Artistry," *National Geographic* 162, 5 (Nov. 1982); J. J. Brody, Catherine J. Scott, and Steven A. LeBlanc, *Mimbres Pottery: Ancient Art of the American Southwest* (Roswell Museum and Art Center, 1983); and J. J. Brody, *Beauty from the Earth: Pueblo Indian Pottery from the University Museum of Archaeology and Anthropology* (University of Pennsylvania, 1990).
2. For more on the art and history of individual pueblos and major artists, see Rick Dillingham, *Acoma and Laguna Pottery* (School of American Research Press, 1992); Barbara Kramer, *Nampeyo and Her Pottery* (University of New Mexico Press, 1996); Francis Harlow and Dwight P. Lanmon, *The Pottery of Zia Pueblo* (School of American Research Press, 2003); and Richard Townsend, ed., *Casas Grandes and The Ceramic Art of the Ancient Southwest*, exh. cat. (Art Institute of Chicago/Yale University Press, 2006).

The Prairie on Fire, pp. 14–15

1. Horatio Greenough to Washington Allston, Apr. 18, 1829, published in *Letters of Horatio Greenough, American Sculptor*, ed. Nathalia Wright (University of Wisconsin Press, 1972), p. 30. The "new year's book" was the annual periodical *The Token: A Christmas and New Year's Present*. The engraving appeared on p. 218.
2. Fisher painted a number of western subjects, listing thirty-six in a notebook that he used to record the works he created after 1825; Mabel Munson Swan, "The Unpublished Notebooks of Alvan Fisher," *Antiques* 68, 2 (Aug. 1955), pp. 126–29. For more on Fisher, see Fred B. Adelson and Jennifer Yunginger Madden, *Seeking the Realization of a Dream: The Paintings of Alvan Fisher*, exh. cat. (Heritage Plantation of Sandwich, 2001); William Dunlap, *History of the Rise and Progress of the Arts of Design in the United States* (1834; repr., Benjamin Blom, 1965),

vol. 2, pp. 32–34; Robert C. Vose, "Alvan Fisher 1792–1863: American Pioneer in Landscape and Genre," *Connecticut Historical Society Bulletin* 27, 4 (Oct. 1962), pp. 104, 107; Edward J. Nygren, *Views and Visions: American Landscape before 1830*, exh. cat. (Corcoran Gallery of Art, 1986); and Fred Adelson, "Alvan Fisher (1792–1863): Pioneer in American Landscape Painting" (Ph.D. diss., Columbia University, 1982).
3. Fisher noted in his diary, "Shall purchase no more prints unless it be some prints from Turner's Paintings as Studies for Style of Landscape painting." Alvan Fisher, diary entry, May 14, 1825, collection of the artist's great-great-great grandson, n.pag., quoted in Adelson and Madden (note 2), pp. xx–xxi.
4. James Fenimore Cooper, *The Prairie; A Tale*, in *The Leatherstocking Tales*, vol. 1 (1827; repr., Library of America, 1985), p. 1160.
5. See, for example, the frontispiece of the first British edition of *The Prairie* (H. Colburn and R. Bentley, 1832).
6. "Scene from Cooper's Novel of the Prairie," in "A Catalogue of Paintings executed after my return from Europe in 1826," vol. 2 (1828), collection of the artist's great-great-great grandson, n.pag. For more on Goodrich, see "Death of S. G. Goodrich, Esq.," *New York Times*, May 11, 1860. *The Prairie on Fire* was first shown in the Boston Athenaeum's annual exhibition in 1829 (cat. 209). Of the twenty-eight works Fisher showed there, eight were owned by Goodrich; see Robert F. Perkins, Jr., and William J. Gavin III, *Boston Athenaeum Art Exhibition Index, 1827–1874* (Library of the Boston Athenaeum, 1980), p. 56.

Three Vases, pp. 16–17

1. The initials ER on the bottom of the vase were recently identified by Grueby expert Susan J. Montgomery as those of Eva Russell, who worked for the firm in 1908 and 1909. For information on Grueby marks and decorators, see Susan J. Montgomery, *The Ceramics of William H. Grueby: The Spirit of the New Idea in Artistic Handicraft* (Arts and Crafts Quarterly Press, 1993), pp. 109–14; and Edwin Atlee Barber, *Marks of American Potters* (Patterson and White, 1904), pp. 99–100.
2. C. Howard Walker, *The Grueby Pottery* (Grueby Faience Company, c. 1900), n.pag. The founder of Detroit's Pewabic Pottery commented, "Unlike many other potteries, there is virtually no mechanical assistance employed and throughout every touch of individual hand work is retained." See Mary Chase Perry, "Grueby Potteries," *Keramic Studio* 2, 12 (Apr. 1901), p. 251.
3. Grueby entered receivership in 1909.
4. For a detailed analysis of Teco's methods, see Susan Stuart Frackelton, "Our American Potteries: Teco Ware," *Sketch Book* 5, 1 (Sept. 1905), pp. 13–19; and Sharon Darling, *Teco: Art Pottery of the Prairie School*, exh. cat. (Erie Art Museum, 1989).
5. For more on Fritz Albert, see Susan Stuart Frackelton, "Our American Potteries: Maratta's and Albert's Work at the Gates Potteries," *Sketchbook* 5, 2 (Oct. 1905), pp. 78–80; and Darling (note 4), pp. 42–43.

5. Gates Potteries, *Hints for Gifts and Home Decoration*, sales cat., 1905, p. 4; and Darling (note 4), pp. 52–53.
7. Herbert J. Hall, "Marblehead Pottery," *Keramic Studio* 10, 2 (June 1908), p. 31. For more on Marblehead, see Marilee Boyd Meyer and Susan J. Montgomery, "Marblehead Pottery: Simplicity and Restraint," *American Ceramic Circle Journal* 14 (2007), pp. 153–74; Jonathan Clancy and Martin Eidelberg, *Beauty in Common Things: American Arts and Crafts Pottery from the Two Red Roses Foundation*, exh. cat. (Two Red Roses Foundation, 2008), pp. 81–93; and idem, "Marblehead Revisited: The Myth of Hannah Tutt," *Style 1900* (Winter 2008/09), pp. 62–69.
8. "The Annual Arts and Crafts Exhibition at the National Arts Club, New York," *Craftsman* 13, 4 (Jan. 1908), p. 482. For additional commentary that compared Marblehead to "some of the best old Japanese pottery," see "Exhibition of the New York Society of Keramic Arts," *Keramic Studio* 11, 2 (June 1909), p. 41.
9. For more on Dow, see Nancy E. Green and Jessie Poesch, *Arthur Wesley Dow and American Arts and Crafts*, exh. cat. (American Federation of Arts, 1999); and Beth Ann and Tommy McPherson, *Arthur Wesley Dow and His Influence upon the Arts and Crafts Movement in America* (Arts and Crafts Press, 1999).

The Room No. VI, pp. 18–19
1. These conditions made the Black Belt the subject of intense scrutiny. Photographers like Russell Lee documented its conditions for the Farm Security Administration, while St. Clair Drake and Horace R. Cayton published their seminal study *Black Metropolis* (Harcourt, Brace and Company, 1945).
2. For more on Cortor, see Romare Bearden and Harry Henderson, *A History of African-American Artists from 1792 to the Present* (Pantheon Books, 1993), pp. 272–79; and *Three Masters: Eldzier Cortor, Hughie Lee-Smith, Archibald John Motley, Jr.*, exh. cat. (Kenkeleba Gallery, 1988). For more on *The Room No. VI* in particular, see Sarah E. Kelly, "*The Room No. VI*" in *American Modernism at the Art Institute of Chicago: From World War I to 1955*, ed. Judith A. Barter (The Art Institute of Chicago/Yale University Press, 2009), cat. 169, pp. 330–34.
3. Cortor also cited a 1941 Art Institute exhibition of French art as being a particular influence. He admired these works' treatment of everyday subjects in an "epic style," a combination that he felt endowed them with gravity and beauty. This was a synthesis that he hoped to achieve in his own work. See *Masterpieces of French Art Lent by the Museums and Collectors of France*, exh. cat. (Art Institute of Chicago, 1941).
4. In June 2007 Cortor described *The Room No. VI* as his showpiece painting, which he intended to have represent him at exhibitions in the late 1940s and early 1950s; Michael Rosenfeld, e-mail to Sarah E. Kelly, June 26, 2007. Curatorial files, Department of American Art.
5. Eldzier Cortor, quoted in *University of Illinois Exhibition of Contemporary American Painting*, exh. cat. (University of Illinois Press, 1951), p. 168.

Okavango Delta Spa, Botswana, pp. 20–21
1. The Durst Lambda printer is a laser-based, large-format device for printing high-resolution images. The digital print illustrated here belongs to a suite of six.
2. For more on Roy, see Joseph Rosa, *Roy: Design Series I*, exh. cat. (San Francisco Museum of Modern Art, 2001); idem, *Figuration in Contemporary Design*, exh. cat. (Art Institute of Chicago/Yale University Press, 2007), pp. 12–13, 48–51; and Kristine Synnes, *Lindy Roy: Architecture of Risk*, Michigan Architecture Papers 11 (University of Michigan, Taubman College of Architecture and Urban Planning, 2004).

New Busan Tower, Busan, South Korea, pp. 22–23
1. For more on Mies and the Glass Skyscraper, see Terence Riley and Barry Bergdoll, eds., *Mies in Berlin* (Museum of Modern Art, New York, 2001); and Phyllis Lambert, *Mies in America* (Abrams, 2001).
2. The digital print illustrated here belongs to a suite of three. The other two show a section and a detail. All measure 61 x 91 cm (24 x 36 in.).
3. For more on PATTERNS, Inc., see Kurt Forster, ed., *METAMORPH: 9th International Architecture Exhibition/Venice Biennale* (Rizzoli, 2004); Joseph Rosa, *Next Generation: Folds, Blobs, +Boxes* (Rizzoli, 2003); idem, ed., *Glamour: Fashion + Industrial Design + Architecture* (San Francisco Museum of Modern Art/Yale University Press, 2004); and idem, *Figuration in Contemporary Design* (Art Institute of Chicago/Yale University Press, 2007), pp. 16–17, 70–73.

Ordos 100, Lot 006, Inner Mongolia, China, pp. 30–31
1. For more on MOS, see Aaron Betsky, ed., *Out There: Architecture Beyond Building, 11th International Architecture Exhibition/Venice Biennale* (Marsilio, 2008); Michael Meredith, ed., *From Control to Design: Parametric/Algorithmic Architecture* (Actar, 2008); and Michael Meredith, ed., *Notes for Those Beginning the Discipline of Architecture* (YouWorkForThem, 2006).

Wine Flask (Hu), pp. 32–33
1. Wine in ancient China was fermented from grain rather than fruit and is more accurately described as millet ale.
2. So pervasive were these changes that they are generally termed the Ritual Reform or Ritual Revolution. For various perspectives on their source, timing, and pace, see Lothar von Falkenhausen, *Chinese Society in the Age of Confucius (1000–250 BC): The Archaeological Evidence* (Cotsen Institute of Archaeology, University of California–Los Angeles, 2006), p. 64; and Edward L Shaughnessy, "Western Zhou History," *The Cambridge History of Ancient China, from the Origins of Civilization to 221 B.C.*, ed. Michael Loewe and Edward L. Shaughnessy (Cambridge University Press, 1999) esp. pp. 323–38. The virtual disappearance of wine vessels may also be explained, at least in part, as a repudiation by Zhou rulers of the indulgent drinking habits of Shang worshippers; see Jessica Rawson, *Western Zhou Ritual Bronzes from the Arthur M. Sackler Collections*, vol. IIA (Arthur M. Sackler Foundation/Arthur M. Sackler Museum, 1990), p. 102. For the stylistic

origin of this form and its place in ritual sets, see Rawson (above), pp 100–02, 105, fig. 147.
3. A medley of stylized birds with cleverly manipulated and distorted features dominated Chinese bronze decoration from c. 975 to c. 850 B.C. For more on their evolution from other zoomorphic motifs, including dragons, see Rawson (note 2), pp. 75–83. The possible significance of these birds eludes modern interpretation.
4. These lids and rings are preserved on a pair of flasks very similar to the Art Institute's in the Nezu Museum, Tokyo. One of the pair is illustrated in *Zhongguo qing tong qi quan qi [Complete Compedium of Chinese Bronzes]* (Wen wu chu ban she, 1998), vol. 6, pl. 133; the other in Rawson (note 2), vol. IIB, p. 611, fig. 95.3. Like many contemporary vessels, the latter flask is cast with an inscription indicating that its commissioners intended it to be passed down through future generations: *Mei Xian makes this treasured hu flask / May for ten thousand years grandsons' grandsons / And son's sons eternally treasure and use [it]*; translation by Edward L. Shaughnessy in an e-mail to Elinor Pearlstein, Apr. 2009.
5. This darkened surface likely accounts for the flask's initial misidentification as a seventeenth- or eighteenth-century version of an ancient vessel when it was auctioned in Germany in 2007. See Kunsthaus Lempertz, Cologne, *Aisatischen Kunst*, sale cat. (Kunsthaus Lempertz, Dec. 7–8, 2007), lot 939. The flask's true age was verified by thermoluminescence testing of its clay core at Oxford Authentication Ltd., on Apr. 25, 2008, and by detailed analysis by conservation scientist Dr. John Twilley. See "Technical and Scientific Examination of a Bronze *Hu* of the Middle Western Zhou Dynasty, 9th Century B.C.," Sept. 4, 2008, curatorial files, Department of Asian Art.

Coin with Portraits of Cleopatra and Mark Antony, pp. 34–35
1. The date and mint of this coin is uncertain. It is thought that these Antony and Cleopatra coins were struck at Antioch, though there is good reason to believe that they were produced further south, in Cleopatra's Phoenician territory. See Numismatica Ars Classica, Zürich, *The Barry Feirstein Collection of Ancient Coins, Part IV, Numismatia Ars Classica*, sale cat. (Numismatica Ars Classica, Apr. 2, 2008), p. 22, lot 55.

Four-Armed Dancing God Ganesha with His Rat Mount, pp. 38–39
1. For images of gilt repoussé and carved wood doorway surrounds see Pratapaditya Pal, ed., *Nepal: Old Images, New Insights*, Marg 56, 2 (Marg Publications/National Centre for the Performing Arts, 2002), pp. 12: 4, 112: 7–9.
2. For a discussion of Ganesha in Nepal, see Mary Shepherd Slusser, *Nepal Mandala: A Cultural Study of the Kathmandu Valley* (Princeton University Press, 1982), vol. 1, pp. 261–63.
3. Ibid. As Nepal and India share a border, many cultural and economic exchanges occurred throughout history. In particular, Nepal's earliest dynasty, the Licchavis (c.

93

300–879 A.D.) claimed to belong to India's Licchavi lineage. See ibid., pp. 12–14, 21, for a discussion of the connection between India and Nepal.

Maharao Guman Singh Riding an Elephant in Procession, pp. 40–41

1. For more on the art of Kota, see Stuart Cary Welch, ed., *Gods, Kings, and Tigers: The Art of Kotah* (Asia Society Galleries/Harvard University Art Museums/Prestel, 1997); and Milo Cleveland Beach, *Rajput Painting at Bundi and Kota* (Artibus Asiae, 1974).
2. M. K. Brijraj Singh, *The Kingdom That Was Kotah: Paintings from Kotah* (Lalit Kala Akademi, 1985), p. 16.
3. Klaus Ebeling, *Ragamala Painting* (Ravi Kumar, 1973) p. 217.
4. Welch (note 1), p. 51.

Blue Phoenix, pp. 42–43

1. This information was adapted from Hans Bjarne Thomsen, "Blue Phoenix," in *Beyond Golden Clouds: Japanese Screens from the Art Institute of Chicago and the Saint Louis Art Museum*, ed. Janice Katz, exh. cat. (The Art Institute of Chicago/Saint Louis Art Museum/Yale University Press, 2009), pp. 180–83.
2. Satō Rinmei, "Dai sankai Teiten kanshōki," *Nihon oyobi Nihonjin* (Nov. 1921), pp. 113–14. The full text is translated in Janice Katz, ed., *Beyond Golden Cloud: Japanese Screens from the Art Institute of Chicago and the Saint Louis Art Museum* (Art Institute of Chicago, 2009), p. 181.

Tableau Vert, pp. 44–45

1. While in Europe, Kelly exhibited his oil works in galleries and museums. He also associated with artist Jean Arp, who introduced him to musician and composer John Cage and to the work of Sophie Taeuber-Arp. These various contacts influenced Kelly's fascination with chance.
2. Ellsworth Kelly, quoted in Diane Waldman, "Ellsworth Kelly," in *Ellsworth Kelly: A Retrospective*, Diane Waldman, ed., exh. cat. (Guggenheim Museum, 1996), p. 17.
3. Paul Taylor, "Ellsworth Kelly: Talking to America's Most Colorful Artist." *Interview* 21, 6 (June 1991), p. 102.
4. As Kelly commented, "The day after I visited Giverny I painted a green picture, a monochrome. I had already done paintings with six different color panels, but now I wondered if I could do a painting with only one color." Accounts differ, however, as to whether the artist painted *Tableau Vert* the first or second day after he returned from Giverny. Ibid. The verso of this work contains the graphite drawing *Study for a Relief (A Paris Wall)*, which Kelly signed and dated 1950.
5. Martin Gayford, "Where the Eye Leads: Ellsworth Kelly Tells Martin Gayford How He Learned to Please Himself," *Modern Painters* 10 (Summer 1997), p. 63.

Da Creepy Lady, pp. 46–47

1. Since 1987 Nutt has focused solely on portraits of women.
2. Whitney Halstead, *Jim Nutt*, exh. cat. (Museum of Contemporary Art, Chicago, 1974), n.pag.

3. In the early 1990s Nutt stopped painting on Plexiglas, instead choosing to work directly on canvas, metal, paper, and wood supports.
4. Jim Nutt, quoted in Franz Schulze, *Fantastic Images: Chicago Art Since 1945* (Follett, 1972), p. 33.
5. Halstead (note 2), n.pag.

Weights and Measures, pp. 48–49

1. Richard Serra, "Weights and Measures," audio guide recording, 2009. Curatorial files, Department of Contemporary Art.
2. Richard Serra, "Steel Props," in *Richard Serra: Sculpture 1985–1998*, ed. Russell Ferguson, Anthony McCall, and Clara Weyergraf-Serra, exh. cat. (Museum of Contemporary Art, Los Angeles/Steidl, 1998), p. 57.

Untitled, pp. 50–51

1. Gober explained the sources for this imagery in the following way: "The hanged man was taken from a political cartoon in Texas, from the late '20s, that I found in a picture collection at the New York Public Library. The sleeping man was from a Sunday ad for Bloomingdales, a sheets ad: a beefcake shot of a guy in bed." "Hanging Man/Sleeping Man: A Conversation between Teresa Bush, Robert Gober, and Ned Rifkin," *Parkett* 27 (1991), p. 93. The two images were first combined as a pattern on an upholstered cushion of a dog bed in *Untitled* (1988).
2. Robert Gober, written statement for the installation of *Untitled* in the Art Institute's Modern Wing, Apr. 13, 2009. Curatorial files, Department of Contemporary Art.

Vignette Suite, pp. 52–53

1. Kerry James Marshall, interview by Lisa Dorin and Tammy Gheith, Aug. 8, 2008.
2. Vignettes are typically modest in size: the form was often used to embellish the title pages and section dividers in books, reaching its fullest expression during the Rococo period in the eighteenth century.
3. Marshall first explored the suite device—and 360-degree rotations of a scene—in five drawings from *Everything Will Be Alright I Just Know It Will* (2004; Museum of Modern Art, New York); Marshall interview (note 1). He completed the original *Vignette* set, which consisted of *Vignettes 2, 3, 4, 5*, and *6*, in 2005 for a solo exhibition at the Camden Arts Center in London. *Vignettes 4, 5*, and *6* are now in private collections. *Vignettes 2* and *3*, the only works from the original five to depict the same couple, were always meant to become part of another, distinct suite. Once these two canvases returned from display, Marshall began work on *Vignettes 2.25, 2.50*, and *2.75*. However, he did not have room in his studio to complete the new paintings with the original two present, so he instead worked from drawings and sketches. For practical purposes, the artist changed the support from Plexiglas to polyvinyl, which weighs roughly one-third less.
4. Marshall interview (note 1).

Hinoki, pp.54–55

1. Charles Ray, written statement for the installation of *Hinoki* in the Art Institute's Modern Wing, Apr. 7, 2009. Curatorial files, Department of Contemporary Art.
2. Ibid.
3. The artist stated, "I realized then that the wood, like the original log, had a life of its own, and I was finally able to let my project go and hopefully breathe life into the world that surrounds it." Ibid.

The Whitfield Cup, pp. 56–57

1. John Whitfield, will dated 1687, Canterbury Cathedral Archives, Kent, England, copy on file in the Department of European Decorative Art.
2. Ibid.
3. Christie's, London, *Highly Important Silver from the Collection of Lord Harris of Peckham*, sale cat. (Christie's, Nov. 25, 2008), pp. 119–24, lot 55.

Side Chair, pp. 58–59

1. Stirling prominently featured this chair in his London sitting room. He was so partial to it, in fact, that he included it in a presentation drawing of the lobby for his Olivetti Headquarters in the New Town of Milton Keynes, and drew himself sitting in it. The chair remained in his home until March 2009, when it was acquired from his widow by the Art Institute of Chicago.
2. James Stirling, quoted in Mark Girouard, *Big Jim: The Life and Work of James Stirling* (Chatto and Windus, 1998), p. 198.

Wall Clock, pp. 60–61

1. As the leading authority on the firm, Roberto Polo, recently noted in April 2008 in an e-mail to Christopher Monkhouse, "During the nineteenth century, [l'Escalier de Cristal] was the most important and fashionable luxury shop in Paris, probably in the world, and specialized in furniture and crystal objects mounted in bronze. In the same tradition of the French eighteenth century "marchand mercier," in its workshops, it assembled and edited the pieces which it subsequently sold in its shop. The Escalier de Cristal was a tastemaker."
2. Edward Strahan [Earl Shinn], *Mr. Vanderbilt's House and Collection*, vol. 3 (George Barrie, 1883–84), p. 59 (ill.).

Apollo and Marsyas, pp. 62–63

1. *Apollo and Marsyas* and the two other paintings (whose present locations are unknown) are illustrated in Henry Thode, *Hans Thoma: Des Meisters Gemälde in 874 Abbildungen* (Stuttgart, 1909), pp. 239, 258. The piece shown on p. 258 also has a painted frame.
2. Writing to a friend in the spring of 1889, Thoma remarked that he had worked "very hard this winter" on three paintings, one of which is "Apollo and Marsyas in [Adolf von] Hildebrand's Campo at the top of the hill under the young cypresses." Hermann Eris Busse, "Hans Thoma–Sein Leben" in *Hans Thoma: Sein Leben in Selbstzeugnissen, Briefen und Berichten*, ed. Hermann Eris Busse (Propyläen Verlag, 1943), p. 152.

1. For more on this collection, see Janusz A. Ostrowski, Karol Lanckoronski (1848–1933)—Polish Connoisseur and Friend of Art," *Studies in Ancient Art and Civilization* 6 (1993), esp. pp. 60–64; Laurie Stein, appendix A, Apr. 25 and Sept. 19, 2008, curatorial files, Department of Medieval to Modern European Painting and Sculpture.

Earthly Paradise, pp. 64–65

1. The cabinet is probably the "sculpture" that Bernard's sister Madeline referred to in a letter she wrote him shortly after leaving Pont-Aven. See Belinda Thomson, *Gauguin's Vision*, exh. cat (National Galleries of Scotland, 2005), p. 79. It is unclear whether Bernard and Gauguin embarked on the cabinet as a personal exercise in painterly carving or whether it was a commissioned project.

2. Bernard's choice of imagery is very close to motifs in the woodcuts he was working on at this time, and it was he who taught Gauguin lithography. Both men repeated similar subjects in the zincographs they exhibited at the Café Volpini on the grounds of the 1889 Universal Exposition in Paris, where their work influenced the next generation of artists, including the Nabis.

Frog-Man (Le Grenouillard), pp. 66–67

1. Philippe Thiébaut "A propos d'un groupe cérmiqueu de Jean Carriès: *Le Grenouillard*," *La revue du Louvre*, (1982), p. 126 nn. 57–58.

2. Jean-Joseph Carriès, as quoted and translated in Charles Janoray, *Symbolism and the Grotesque: The Fantastical Creatures of Carriès and Ringel d'Illzach and Other Artists* (Charles Janoray, 2006), p. 4.

Still Life Filled with Space, pp. 68–69

1. Amédée Ozenfant and Charles-Édouard Jeanneret, *Après le cubisme* (Edition des Commentaires, 1918), p. 11; English translation from Carol S. Eliel, *L'Esprit nouveau: Purism in Paris, 1918–1925*, exh. cat. (Los Angeles County Museum of Art/Abrams, 2001), p. 132.

2. Ozenfant and Jeanneret (note 1), p. 59; English translation from Eliel (note 1), p. 165. Although Le Corbusier contended that his first painting was *La Cheminée* (1918; Fondation Le Corbusier, Paris), a work informed by the Purist aesthetic, he executed a few earlier paintings and watercolors that were largely informed by the work of Paul Cézanne as well as by Cubism, Fauvism, Art Nouveau, and even German Expressionism. See Françoise Ducros, "From Art Nouveau to Purism: Le Corbusier and Painting," in *Le Corbusier Before Le Corbusier: Applied Arts, Architecture, Painting, Photography 1907–1922*, ed. Stanislaus von Moos and Arthur Rüegg, exh. cat. (Yale University Press/Bard Graduate Center/Langmatt Museum, 2002), p. 133.

3. Le Corbusier was so involved with his collaborations with Ozenfant between 1918 and 1922 that he did not build anything, and one of the few architectural projects he did execute between 1922 and 1925 was a studio residence for Ozenfant; Eliel (note 1), pp. 22–23.

4. Naïma Jornod and Jean-Pierre Jornod include a second title for the work, *Nature morte limpide (Transparent Still Life)*; see *Le Corbusier (Charles Edouard Jeanneret): Catalogue raisonné de l'oeuvre peint*, vol. 1 (Skira, 2005), cat. 43, pp. 387–88.

5. Eliel (note 1), p. 25.

6. Ibid., p. 54.

Object, pp. 70–71

1. Since Cahun's work was rediscovered in the 1980s, it has been the subject of much scholarship, including François Leperlier, *Claude Cahun, l'écart et la métamorphose* (Jean-Michel Place, 1992); Louise Downie, ed., *Don't Kiss Me: The Art of Claude Cahun and Marcel Moore* (Tate Publishing/Jersey Heritage Trust, 2006); and Gen Doy, *Claude Cahun: A Sensual Politics of Photography* (I. B. Tauris, 2007).

2. Cahun's theatrical self-portraits have often been heralded as precursors to the work of recent photographers including Nan Goldin and Cindy Sherman. Cahun also experimented with other artistic media, often in collaboration with her lifelong partner Suzanne Malherbe (known as Marcel Moore). Born in Nantes, Cahun settled in Paris with Moore in the early 1920s. In 1938 they relocated to the island of Jersey, where, after the outbreak of World War II and the invasion of German troops, they engaged in—and were arrested for—anti-war activities.

3. The 1936 exhibition catalogue lists only two objects by Cahun: *Un air de famille* and *Souris valseuses*. Descriptions of these works can be found in Doy (note 1), p. 124. The third untitled and uncatalogued piece—the one that is the subject of this entry—is visible in an installation photograph of the 1936 exhibition and was first identified as Cahun's in the 1986 Zabriskie Gallery exhibition catalogue, *1936 Surrealism*. See Steven Harris, *Surrealist Art and Thought in the 1930s: Art, Politics, and Psyche* (Cambridge University Press, 2004), pp. 163, 281 n. 44.

4. Some of the hair is human; the rest is either artificial or from an animal.

5. As detailed in Harris (note 3) pp. 168–73, this phrase unites two unrelated sources—the first a well-known slogan from France's left-wing Popular Front, and the second a line printed on Belgian currency. With this conflated text, Cahun referenced contemporary politics and pointed an accusatory finger at the supposed revolutionary leaders of France.

6. A *bilboquet* is a toy with a ball on a string attached to a cup or spike. Cahun's *Object* probably also references Georges Bataille's novel *Histoire de l'Oeil* (1928), which details the sexual exploits and perversions of two young lovers. Harris (note 3), among others, has identified these various iconographical sources. For a psychoanalytical reading of Cahun's *Object*, see Harris (note 3), pp. 163–73.

7. Claude Cahun, "Prenez garde aux objets domestiques," *Cahiers d'Art* 11 (1936), p. 46. This essay was included in a special issue of *Cahiers d'Art* that coincided with the 1936 *Surrealist Exposition of Objects*. For this English translation and a discussion of the essay, see Harris (note 3), pp. 160–63, 178–80. Cahun's article is interrupted by a full page photograph (attributed to Willy Eggarter) of a disembodied hand holding a large egg from the ostrich-like epiornis; see Cahun (above), p. 47. The formal similarities between the subject matter of Cahun's *Object* and of this photograph of a scientific specimen—one of the "natural objects" included in the 1936 exhibition—are noteworthy.

8. I would like to thank Art Institute curator Stephanie D'Alessandro for sharing her research on this piece, and for providing guidance during the writing of this entry.

Self-Portrait with Camera, pp. 72–73

1. "Mr. Steichen's Pictures," *Photographic Art Journal* 2, 14 (London, Apr. 15, 1902), pp. 27–28.

2. Edward Steichen, "291," *Camera Work* 47 (Jan. 1915), p. 65.

Satiric Dancer, pp. 74–75

1. Sarah Greenough, "To Become a Virgin Again," in Sarah Greenough, Robert Gurbo, and Sarah Kennel, *André Kertész*, exh. cat. (National Gallery of Art, Washington, D.C., 2005), p. 67.

2. Paul Dermée, "Frère voyant [Brother Seeing-Eye]," 1927, published in *Photo-Kertész Exposition*, exh. cat. (Galerie Au Sacre du Printemps, 1928); repr. in French and English in *Stranger to Paris: Au Sacre du Printemps Galerie*, 1927 (Jane Corkin Gallery, 1992), p. 15 (translation modified).

3. Hermann Ungar, "Kleine Lügen: Dialog zwischen Eheleuten," *Die Dame* (Oct. 1927), p. 2. It is possible that the photograph, which Kertész dated to 1926, was created only in 1927, and perhaps even under the impulse of Ungar's text. Beőthy's sculpture is dated 1927 by his heirs; see www.istvanbeothy.fr (site accessed July 2009). The sculptor repaid Kertész's interest with his own homage to the photographer, in an etching that is also dated 1927; see Greenough, Gurbo, and Kennel (note 1), p. 69. Brassaï's widow also recalled in a conversation with David Travis that the photograph was from 1927; "A. K. From Paris to New York," 1984–85, exhibition files, box 5, folder marked "Xerox Images," Art Institute of Chicago Archives.

4. See, for example, annual price lists from 1976 and 1980 to 1982; "André Kertész," artist files, folder 2, Department of Photography.

Study for "Let's Return the Country's Coal Debt" and Worker Men and Women: Everyone Vote in the Soviet Elections, pp. 76–77

1. Maria Gough provides a detailed historical review of the theoretical debates that gave rise to Constructivism in 1920 and 1921; see *The Artist as Producer: Russian Constructivism in Revolution* (University of California Press, 2005).

2. Cited as paraphrase in Margarita Tupitsyn, *Gustav Klutsis and Valentina Kulagina: Photography and Montage after Constructivism* (International Center of Photography/Steidl, 2004), p. 37.

Near Jackson, Mississippi, pp. 78–79

1. Janet Malcolm, "Color," *New Yorker* 53, 34 (Oct. 10, 1977), p. 107. Malcolm wrote that, in comparison to Photorealist paintings, artistic color photography looked "insignificant, dull, even tacky, on the wall." Ibid., pp. 107–08.

2. John Szarkowski, untitled essay, in *William Eggleston's Guide* (Museum of Modern Art/MIT Press, 1976), p. 14.

3. Richard B. Woodward, "Memphis Beau," *Vanity Fair* (London, Oct. 1991), pp. 215–20, 238, 240–41, 244–45.

4. These prints will be featured in the Art Institute's spring 2010 installation of the artist's first retrospective exhibition in the United States, *William Eggleston: Democratic Camera, Photographs and Video, 1961–2008*. This exhibition was organized by the Whitney Museum of American Art, New York, in association with Haus der Kunst, Munich.

The Nativity and Coffer, pp. 80–81

1. For more on this sale, see Pierre Bergé, Paris, *Collection Marie-Thérèse et André Jammes: coffrets de messages, images du Moyen Âge et traditions populaires*, sale cat. (Pierre Bergé, Nov. 7, 2007), pp. 40–41 (ill.), lot 17.

2. I would like to thank the following Art Institute colleagues for their help and collaboration in researching this acquisition: Emily Heye, Suzanne Karr Schmidt, Kim Nichols, Christina Nielsen, and Martha Wolff. Elsewhere, Sandra Hindman, Armin Kunz, and Paul Saenger also offered valuable assistance.

3. Sandra Hindman, in *Pen to Press/Paint to Print: Manuscript Illumination and Early Prints in the Age of Gutenberg* (Les Enluminures, 2009), pp. 54–55, discusses the possibility that stationers and printers were involved with the manufacture of these coffers, citing as evidence the stationer "Jean Bezard," whose name has been found twice on prints adorning boxes.

4. This artist is also identified as the Master of the Apocalypse Rose for his design of the great rose window for Sainte Chapell, Paris. See Ina Nettekoven, *Der Meister der Apocalypsenrose der Sainte Chapell und die Pariser Buchkunst um 1500*, Ars Nova 9 (Brepols, 2004). He may have been Jean d'Ypres, now considered one of the major French artists of the period.

5. Richard S. Field, ed., *The Illustrated Bartsch* (Abaris Books, 1987), vol. 161, pp. 93–95, no. 63; see also Wilhelm Schreiber, *Handbuch der Holz- und Metallschnitte des XV. Jahrhundert* (Leipzig, 1926–30), vol. 8, nos. 63a–c; and Richard S. Field, *Fifteenth Century Woodcuts and Metalcuts from the National Gallery of Art* (National Gallery of Art, Washington, D.C., 1965), no. 8.

6. While their shape and size originally suggested to scholars that these objects started as safety boxes for devotional and liturgical books, some writers also hypothesized that they were employed for transporting correspondence or as alms boxes. The presence of iron bands shaped like belt loops on the sides of many boxes suggest that smaller examples could have been worn on the belt, and heavier boxes carried on the messenger's back, on a saddle, or strapped to luggage.

7. Séverine Lepape, Bibliothèque Nationale de France, Paris (which has the largest known collection of *coffrets*), and Michel Huynh, Musée National du Moyen Age (Cluny), Paris, are collaborating on a comprehensive study of more than 80 boxes (forthcoming in 2009), to be followed by an exhibition; see also *Fifteenth-Century Woodcuts in French Late-Gothic Coffrets* (C. G. Boerner/Les Enluminures/Helmut H. Rumbler, 2008); and

Peter Parshall and Rainer Schoch, *Origins of European Printmaking: Fifteenth Century Woodcuts and their Public*, exh cat. (National Gallery of Art, Washington, D.C., and Germanisches Nationalmuseum, 2005), pp. 171–73, cat. 42.

8. Many safety boxes show signs of having been lovingly restored over the centuries.

Academic Study of a Reclining Male Nude, pp. 82–83

1. This handsome model has been identified as Jean-François Deschamps (died 1773), who worked at the Royal Academy in Paris from 1725 to 1773.

2. Pierre Rosenberg observed this dichotomy in James Rubin's pioneering study, *Eighteenth-Century French Life-Drawing: Selections from the Collection of Mathias Polakovits* (Princeton Art Museum, 1977), pp. 10–11.

3. Françoise Joullie to Michel Gierzod, June 5, 2001, on file in the Department of Prints and Drawings.

4. A third similar drawing was sold at Sotheby's, New York, Jan. 28, 1998, lot 215, and now belongs to a Mrs. Berger, according to Alastair Lang who, along with Françoise Jolie, considers it a copy; see Joullie to Gierzod (note 3).

5. In the Louvre sheet (RF 31880), the model's left knee is up; his right arm is bent with his hand holding his chin rather than resting on a book; and his left arm is extended. The background shadow is described in the strong regular parallel lines characteristic of so many academic male figure drawings, but, as in the Chicago study, the figure itself is delineated with long sweeping contours and swelling muscles.

6. This work was once in the distinguished collections of the Marquis de Chennevières and Baron Roger Portalis, and was acquired by the Galerie Cailleux in 1964. Close observation suggests that the objects are materials used by artists to smear chalks for atmospheric effects.

7. For example, the Chicago sheet was undoubtedly the first elaboration and alteration of the Louvre sheet, as it shares the use of elongated contour lines to define the figure's right calf; the Canadian work introduces more prominent parallel hatching strokes.

8. The sheet's greater use of stumping suggests that Boucher was demonstrating the range of effects possible with the three-chalk technique.

9. The catalogue of his sale on Dec. 3, 1781, lists simply "Une autre Académie, représentant un Homme nud couché sur une Pierre, aux crayons noir & blanc"; Hotel de Bullion, Paris, *Catalogue des tableaux et dessins précieux qui composent le Cabinet de M. de Sireul* (Hotel de Bullion, Dec. 3, 1781), p. 48, lot 219. The Art Institute's *académie* is in its original eighteenth century mount, which is inscribed *fragile / à Madame (Verger) / à Dèves / fragile* in pen and brown ink on the back.

Bathers, pp. 84–85

1. Describing this mission in his artistic credo in 1927, Beckmann stated, "The artist in the contemporary sense is the conscious shaper of the transcendent idea. . . . His activity is of vital significance to the state, since it is he that established the boundaries of a new culture." Max Beckmann, "The Artist in the State," *Europäische Revue*

(1927) repr. in *Max Beckmann: Self-Portrait in Words. Collected Writings and Statements, 1903–1950*, ed. Barbara Copeland Buenger (University of Chicago Press, 1997), p. 287.

2. For more on Beckmann's bather pictures, see Klaus Gallwitz and Ortrud Westheider, eds., *Max Beckmann: Menschen am Meer* (Hatje Cantz, 2003).

3. For an image of this photograph, see Sean Rainbird, ed., *Max Beckmann* (Tate Publishing, 2003), p. 271. One scholar has suggested that the figure in the black bathing cap in the Chicago drawing is Beckmann himself; see Fritz Erpel, *Max Beckmann: Leben im Werk, die Selbstbildnisse* (Beck, 1985), p. 337, cat. 132A, fig. 128.

Untitled 6/20/89, pp. 85–86

1. Roberta Smith, "Drawing from Within," in *Amerikanische Zeichnungen in den achtziger Jahren*, ed. Rolf Wedewer, exh. cat. (F. Jahn, 1990), p. 13.

2. Included in the twenty works are two independent series of seven sheets each, one in blue ballpoint pen and the other in graphite.

3. Hilarie M. Sheets, "An 'Art World Secret' Plumbs the Mysterious Id," *New York Times*, Oct. 27, 2002.

4. Like Guston, Dunham's imagery has become more representational as it has matured. Just as *Untitled 6/20/89* exemplifies his style from the late 1980s, *The Search for Orgone: Drawing #1* (2001)—acquired with *Untitled 6/20/89*—typifies the artist's more figurative recent manner. It depicts his alter ego: a top-hatted man with bulbous eyes, angular mouth and teeth, and penis nose.

Panel, pp. 86–87

1. Virginia Gardner Troy, *Rug* (Henry Regnery Company, 1974), p. 24.

2. Ibid., p. 14.

3. For other examples, see Bath (note 1), p. 24; Erich Meyer-Heisig, *Weberei Nadelwerk Zeugdruck* (Prestel, 1956), figs. 68–69; and Donna Ghelerter et al., *A Catalogue of Exquisite and Rare Works of Art, including 17th to 20th Century Costume Textiles and Needlework, Winter 2008–2009*, sale cat. (Cora Ginsburg), pp. 14–15.

4. Arthur Lotz, *Bibliographie der Modelbücher: Beschreibendes Verzeichnis der Stick- und Spitzenmusterbücher des 16. und 17. Jahrhunderts* (K. W. Hiersemann, 1933), pp. 35–111.

Ceremonial Skirt Cloth (Dodot), pp. 90–91

1. Mary Hunt Kahlenberg, "Cloth Currency," *Hali* 154 (Winter 2007), pp. 69, 70.

2. Mattiebelle Gittinger, *Master Dyers to the World, Technique and Trade in Early Indian Dyed Cotton Textiles* (Textile Museum, 1982), pp. 19–20, 23.

3. Robyn Maxwell, *Textiles of Southeast Asia: Tradition, Trade and Transformation* (Periplus, 2003), pp. 205, 273.

4. Kahlenberg (note 1), p. 72.

5. Robyn Maxwell, *Sari to Sarong: Five Hundred Years of Indian and Indonesian Textile Exchange* (National Gallery of Australia, 2003), p. 115.

6. Kahlenberg (note 1), p. 74.